FOOD

FOUNTAINHEAD PRESS V SERIES

Edited by
Brooke Rollins and Lee Bauknight

FOUNTAINHEAD
PRESS

Our green initiatives include:

Electronic Products
We deliver products in non-paper form whenever possible. This includes pdf downloadables, flash drives, & CDs.

Electronic Samples
We use Xample, a new electronic sampling system. Instructor samples are sent via a personalized web page that links to pdf downloads.

FSC Certified Printers
All of our printers are certified by the Forest Service Council which promotes environmentally and socially responsible management of the world's forests. This program allows consumer groups, individual consumers, and businesses to work together hand-in-hand to promote responsible use of the world's forests as a renewable and sustainable resource.

Recycled Paper
Most of our products are printed on a minimum of 30% post-consumer waste recycled paper.

Support of Green Causes
When we do print, we donate a portion of our revenue to green causes. Listed below are a few of the organizations that have received donations from Fountainhead Press. We welcome your feedback and suggestions for contributions, as we are always searching for worthy initiatives.
Rainforest 2 Reef
Environmental Working Group

Design by Susan Moore

Editorial Assistance from Eme Crawford

Cover Artwork, "The Blue Delft Burger" by Marcella Lassen

Copyright © 2010 by Fountainhead Press

All rights reserved. No part of this book may be reproduced or utilized in any form or by any means, electronic or mechanical, including photocopying and recording, or by any informational storage and retrieval system without written permission from the publisher.

Books may be purchased for educational purposes.

For information, please call or write:

1-800-586-0330

Fountainhead Press
Southlake, TX 76092

Web Site: www.fountainheadpress.com
E-mail: customerservice@fountainheadpress.com

First Edition

ISBN: 978-1-59871-431-9

Printed in the United States of America

INTRODUCTION TO THE FOUNTAINHEAD PRESS V SERIES

By Brooke Rollins and Lee Bauknight
Series Editors

The *Fountainhead Press V Series* is a new collection of single-topic readers that takes a unique look at some of today's most pressing issues. Designed to give writing students a more nuanced introduction to public discourse—on the environment, on food, and on digital life, to name a few of the topics—the books feature writing, research, and invention prompts that can be adapted to nearly any kind of college writing class. Each *V Series* textbook focuses on a single issue and includes multi-genre and multimodal readings and assignments that move the discourse beyond the most familiar patterns of debate—patterns usually fettered by entrenched positions and often obsessed with "winning."

The ultimate goal of the series is to help writing students—who tend to hover on the periphery of public discourse—think, explore, find their voices, and skillfully compose texts in a variety of media and genres. Not only do the books help students think about compelling issues and how they might address them, they also give students the practice they need to develop their research, rhetorical, and writing skills. Together, the readings, prompts, and longer assignments show students how to add their voices to the conversations about these issues in meaningful and productive ways.

With enough readings and composing tasks to sustain an entire quarter or semester, and inexpensive enough to be used in combination with other rhetorics and readers, the *Fountainhead Press V Series* provides instructors with the flexibility to build the writing courses they want and need to teach. An instructor interested in deeply exploring environmental issues, for example, could design a semester- or quarter-long course using *Green*, the first of the *V Series* texts. On the other hand, an instructor who wanted to teach discrete units on different issues could use two or more of the *V Series* books. In either case, the texts would give students ample opportunity—and a variety of ways—to engage with the issues at hand.

The *V Series* uses the term "composition" in its broadest sense. Of course, the textbooks provide students plenty of opportunities to write, but they also include assignments that take students beyond the page. Books in the series encourage students to explore other modes of communication by prompting them to design web sites, for example; to produce videos, posters, and presentations; to conduct primary and secondary research; and to develop projects with community partners that might incorporate any number of these skills. Ultimately, we have designed the *Fountainhead Press V Series* to work for teachers and students. With their carefully chosen readings, built-in flexibility, and sound rhetorical grounding, the *V Series* books would be a dynamic and user-friendly addition to any writing class.

TABLE OF CONTENTS

INTRODUCTION
RECIPE WRITING

BY BROOKE ROLLINS

STEAMED MARYLAND BLUE CRABS

3 cups water
2 bottles of beer (use a pale lager or an American style ale)
1 cup white vinegar
1 cup Old Bay seasoning
1/4 cup + 2 tbsp of rock salt or coarse sea salt
24 live Maryland blue crabs
Serves 4 to 6

1. In a medium bowl, combine Old Bay seasoning and salt, set aside.
2. In an extra large stock pot fitted with a steaming rack, combine water, beer, and vinegar, and bring to a boil. Make sure that the rack is raised 6 to 8 inches from the bottom of the pot so that the crabs do not touch the boiling liquid (you can use bricks to raise the rack, if necessary).
3. Using tongs (the crabs will pinch bare hands), layer crabs on the steaming rack and generously shower the spice mixture over each layer. Reserve a scant quarter cup of the spice mixture for serving.
4. Cover the pot tightly, and place a heavy brick on the lid to prevent crabs from escaping.
5. Boil over high heat until crabs are a bright orangey red, about 30-35 minutes.
6. Serve on a newspaper-covered table with wooden mallets, paring knives, drawn butter, and the remaining spice mixture.

A recipe is a set of instructions, properly ordered and formatted according to familiar constraints. Almost entirely oriented toward helping its user perform a task (perhaps for the first time, perhaps for the four-hundredth), the genre is above all functional. Located at the very top, the title of the dish allows the cook to organize the recipe according to type: appetizers, sides, main courses, meats, seafood, desserts, and the like. The text that follows lists every ingredient needed to begin and then provides a step-by-step procedure for bringing the dish to completion. It even suggests how to and how many might enjoy what's just been created, all written in as economical a language as possible.

But beyond the economy and the instruction-manual style prose, a recipe does much more. It weaves a narrative full of color, taste, texture, and sound. It promises reward and evokes indelible memories. It alludes to a coming sensual experience, one possibly shared with family and friends. Like an engrossing novel, a recipe opens by setting a scene. It moves through differentiated stages of incompletion (perhaps even adventure) and then resolves the tension with a satisfying—if predictable—conclusion, hinting towards the pleasurable experience of having completed something and of enjoying the rewards of this labor.

The story that this recipe tells is of my childhood. I grew up in south central Pennsylvania, just 30 miles north of the Maryland border, and eating Chesapeake Bay blue crabs—so named for the beautiful blue hue on their legs—was a summer tradition that connected our family to my grandmother's Baltimore roots. From net to table, blue crabs offered adventures that even today—nearly 30 years after my first encounter with them—tie me to my family and my home.

In part because this recipe includes live quarry, the act of preparing the meal involved a certain amount of risk. True to their name, crabs do not possess a yielding or pleasant demeanor, and the last thing they want to do is enter a cauldron for the steam to end all steams. So, rather than placing the angry fare into the pot with bare hands, we had to use tongs—the surrogate version of the crabs' own small but powerful pincers. Without them, our hands were vulnerable to their pointed, fine-toothed claws. And beyond this possibility of injury, there was the none-too-small matter of actually killing dinner ourselves. Having mustered the nerve to deliver the crabs to their final destination, we were a bit jarred to discover that the captives near the top of the steamer had found the strength to dismantle the lid and make a break for freedom. Eventually we learned to put a heavy brick on the lid, preventing the otherwise inevitable escapes.

Despite all of this excitement, cooking the crabs was just the start of the experience—a unique challenge lay in store once the meal hit the newspaper-covered table. After the longest 30-minutes of my young life, we removed the tightly sealed lid to see that the crabs' beautiful blue-green shells had been transformed into a vivid rusty red. We turned the crabs out onto the middle of the table and began the feast, which was far more than a simple act of eating: it was an hours-long celebration of the arrival of summer.

Eating a steamed blue crab is anything but simple. In fact, I would hazard that the sublime deliciousness of its meat is directly proportional to the difficulty of accessing it. The ultimate prize is the meat of the backfin—the place where the crab's back swimming legs meet its body. Here you'll find the most succulent meat with the most consistent and dense texture. But this I would always save for last. It was the reward for expertly removing—sometimes with my bare hands, sometimes with my paring knife and wooden mallet, sometimes with my teeth—all of the meat from every joint of the crab's spidery legs and from every crevice of its side body.

Picking crabs is a game of patience and precision, and because it can take hours to make your way through a whole meal's worth, the practice allows for that rare and comfortable sort of family bonding that can only occur in the midst of a shared project. Our project while eating crabs was to get every last bit of meat they had to offer. Even then—in the early 1980s—the Chesapeake Bay had suffered environmental damage, and the crabs were in such demand that they were often over harvested. We couldn't have them often, and that they were a rare treat made expert picking all the more important.

The aftermath of a crab feast is an epic mess, and it usually comes with a vague feeling of hunger—blue crabs don't have all that much meat to offer, and if you spread the eating out over several hours it's possible to emerge feeling ready for dinner. Covered with small paper-like cuts from the occasional unyielding shell, our hands burned from the spice, and the carnage left on the table (including discarded shells, scraped out gills or "devil's fingers," and left behind digestive tracts) is something that no food magazine would ever feature in a color spread. And yet I can attest that to survey this ostensibly unpalatable scene is to know that you have eaten well.

That I learned at age six a process that's about as complicated as driving a car is something I'm still strangely proud of. I've lived in several different parts of the country since leaving home, and one constant is that I can pick a crab as well as anyone on the Eastern Seaboard. This single recipe connects me to a lifetime of memories, binds me to a locale, and ties me to my family. Yet it is merely a gesture toward the singularly important place that food holds in our lives. Far more than providing sustenance, food defines us. It connects us with people and places. It sets us in relation to others. It calls up important questions of sustainability and production, of ethics and responsibility.

For all these reasons, food gives us a variety of rich opportunities for writing and research, and we have designed this book so that you might read, think, and compose with all of these considerations and questions in mind. We open *Food* with a piece called "The Cooking Ape," an interview with anthropologist Richard Wrangham, who argues that mastering fire and using it to cook played a central role in our evolution. Against this backdrop, we hope you will see in the collection of readings and images a complex yet entirely accessible narrative about the variety of ways that food sustains, inspires, and shapes us. This narrative is woven together from personal stories about growing, preparing, and eating food; from reflections about restaurants and celebrity chefs; and from reports on and arguments about the politics of food.

In addition to these written and visual texts, *Food* includes research, invention, and composing prompts that will help you add your voice to the ongoing conversations about a variety of food-related issues. As you read the selections and work through the corresponding prompts, we hope you will keep an eye trained beyond the page. Indeed, many of the prompts will allow you to link up, not only with your classmates, but also with multi-genre texts and ongoing food, farm, restaurant, and food media related projects. And you'll be doing more than writing here: prompts and other assignments in the book will encourage you to explore various modes of communication—by asking you to write scripts and produce videos, for example; to develop presentations; to conduct primary and secondary research; and to analyze and explain menus and food production practices.

One good way to get started would be to try out the slice of life assignment below. Begin your writing about food by doing some "recipe writing" of your own. Choose a recipe from your own life and explore the ways that food helps define you.

Begin by finding a favorite family recipe (call home, look in your family recipe box or file folder, or remember a meal that you or one of your family members prepared regularly and write it into recipe form with the help of some online research). Once you've found your recipe, place it at the beginning of a new document and think of it as a starting place—the first few lines of a vivid story you will tell. From there, illustrate and bring to life the implied narrative of the recipe in essay form. Look to each formulaic element of the recipe and think about amplifying each of these elements in your essay:

- **RECIPE TITLE:** Does the title point to a specific place, context, or ingredient that means something to you?

- **NUMBER OF PEOPLE SERVED:** In the context of your life and experience, who are the people eating this dish (or who might they be)? How do you remember or imagine this group of people together as they eat the meal? What are their relationships to each other? How do these people come together over food? What role does the food play in bringing them together?

- **INGREDIENT LIST:** What materials and ingredients do you need to complete the recipe? What sensual elements do you see here? What are the sights, tastes, smells, and sounds hiding in this simple list? Are there any unique components you need to explain to an outside audience?

- **SERVING SUGGESTIONS:** How is this meal served? Describe the look, smell, and taste, and point out the small details. (For example, what dishes were used to serve it? Did you eat it inside or outside?) Think, too, of the individuals eating the meal. Where were they sitting? Do they enjoy it? Hate it? Is it new to them? What are the interesting responses?

Once you have developed notes based on these invention suggestions, write an essay that vividly dramatizes and tells the story of your recipe to an audience who did not experience the meal with you. In other words, write an essay that invites us to your table. Write an essay that uses these elements of the recipe to tell readers something about you.

Elisabeth Townsend writes about food, wine, and travel for The Boston Globe *and other newspapers and magazines. She conducted the following interview with primatologist Richard Wrangham in 2005 for* Gastronomica: The Journal of Food and Culture. *Wrangham's book* Catching Fire: How Cooking Made Us Human—The Cooking Ape *was a working title—was published in 2009.*

excerpts from

THE COOKING APE

BY ELISABETH TOWNSEND

Primatologist Richard Wrangham might be best known for the 1996 book he coauthored with writer Dale Peterson, *Demonic Males: Apes and the Origins of Human Violence*, where he used his research on intergroup aggression in chimpanzees to reflect on combative male behavior. Wrangham's twenty-five years of research have always been based on a deep interest in human evolution and behavior, and recently he's shifted his focus to the evolution of cooking in humans.

An anthropology professor at Harvard University, Wrangham, fifty-six, was first mesmerized by Africa when he spent a year working in Kafue National Park in western Zambia before going to college. There, he assisted a research biologist in studying the behavior and ecology of the waterbuck, falling "in love with the excitement of finding out about African habitats and species." He's been back to Africa every year since then, with only one exception— the year his first son was born.

Though Wrangham has made his reputation explaining the similarities and differences across species in primate social organizations, he expects that his work on cooking will

Richard Wrangham
Photo by Jim Harrison

have the broadest impact because cooking affects many human behaviors—such as those associated with food choice, familial relationships, and food production that can satisfy a huge world population. His favorite part of the day is when he can steal an hour from teaching to analyze chimp data or to work on his new book, *The Cooking Ape*. But Wrangham is happiest at his Ugandan research site, enjoying those quiet moments alone with the chimps, watching their relationships and catching up on the social gossip. He hasn't eaten a mammal since 1976 because of his profound empathy for the ones he has enjoyed and spent so much time with in the wild. Occasionally, his vegetarianism makes life a bit harder, as when a host offers him meat, but he'll never turn down seconds on a chocolate roulade. Wrangham spoke from his home in Weston, Massachusettes.

ET: *What prompted your research into how cooking affected human evolution?*

RW: As a Primatologist, I am often asked to think about human evolution. I sat one evening in my living room preparing a lecture for the next day, thinking about the standard story that involved hunting being important around two million years ago. As I was staring at the fire, I had an almost ghostly experience where I just allowed my eyes to be drawn deep into the fire. I could feel around me the presence of hominids, from up to one million years ago, sitting in the African bush.

I started thinking about the fact that fire is something that has been on the Earth ever since there's been plant vegetation and how when I'm in the bush there is no way that I'm going to spend a night without sitting next to a fire. I was thinking about the impact of fire on the "cookability" of food.

Then I thought, "Well, would there really have been a fire for our early ancestors—a million years ago, say?"

I realized I didn't know the answer to the question. But I also realized that it was extremely difficult to imagine that they did not have cooking, because even as long as 1,500,000 years ago humans looked incredibly similar from the neck down to humans living today. Even our heads are very similar—though we have larger brains and we don't have quite as big a mouth or teeth as they did. So surely, if those million-year-old ancestors were generally like us in the size and shape of their bodies, they should have been eating cooked food. After all, cooking has this huge impact. It changes so much about how we relate to the natural environment: it changes the ease with which we digest the food; it changes the availability of calories; and it changes the distribution of food.

If cooking has such a big evolutionary impact, in other words, and we haven't changed much, then there are only two possibilities. Either we somehow managed to adopt cooking without it affecting us very much, which would be very mysterious, or it happened so early that cooking had already been adopted by a million years ago.

ET: *What's an example of how changes in the food supply affected primates and how that led you to think cooking had a significant impact on humans?*

RW: If you compare chimpanzees to gorillas, they eat very similar things. They both like to eat fruits when fruits are available. They both eat more leaves and stems when there aren't many fruits available. But there's one relatively small difference when there's a shortage of fruit, gorillas will switch entirely to eating leaves and stems, whereas chimpanzees absolutely insist on finding their daily ration of fruits before they go bulk up on leaves and stems. That's why gorillas can live entirely without fruit—in the mountains of Uganda, for instance—whereas we don't know of any place where chimpanzees can live entirely without access to fruit.

The small difference in food supply between chimps and gorillas can account for the fact that the gorillas are three to four times the body size of chimpanzees and that they live in more-stable groups. Therefore, gorillas have an entirely different set of sexual relationships, with males being enormously bigger than females, and so on. This is just one example where a relatively small difference in the food supply creates a big difference in the way that two species look and behave. And to shift from eating raw food to eating cooked food is a much bigger change!

ET: *How did cooking change calorie intake and thus the human species?*

RW: Amazingly, we still don't have a good picture of the most important ways in which cooking changes food. There are different effects on plant foods and meat, though. One impact on plant foods is probably to increase digestibility. That means that our food has a relatively low proportion of indigestible materials; in modern surveys you see the 10 percent or less of what we eat is indigestible plant material (fiber, in other words). Whereas in chimpanzees, for instance, fiber is over 30 percent, which therefore seems a reasonable guess for what it might have been like in our raw-food-eating ancestors. Well, if we ate 30 percent fiber, compared with 10 percent now, that 20 percent of the food our ancestors were eating was just bulk material passing through the gut. So, they simply absorbed less energy.

That 20 percent figure is a lot. When we compare the actual rate of energy expenditure in human foragers, which is between 1.5 and 2.2 times the basal metabolic rate, as compared with 1.4 times for chimpanzees, we're getting a lot of extra energy from somewhere compared to the chimpanzees. Where are we getting it from? I think it's because the food that humans are eating is more digestible. Instead of spending all day with our guts holding a high proportion of indigestible material, we're able to have a higher continuous stream of calories going through our guts.

What's the result? Maybe, it explains why humans used so much energy, starting around 1.9 million years ago. First, that's when we got our bigger body, made by the greater amount of energy. Second, it means that we can have a relatively large proportion of expensive organs, such as brains (they're expensive in the sense of using calories at a particularly high rate). For a long time people have been interested in the notion that, since the brain is unusually expensive, our ancestors needed to have some way of getting more energy in order to afford having a bigger brain. At 1.9 million years ago, you have arguably the largest increase in brain size in evolution. Third, there's the opportunity for longer travel distance per day because you just got more energy to put into traveling. Chimpanzees are quite long-distance travelers at 2.5, 3, 4.5 kilometers a day, but humans, males in particular, are traveling 9, 10, 15, 20 kilometers a day—a lot more than chimps.

This extra energy probably comes from the fact that, as a result of cooking, we're able to eat a relatively compact food that is full of calories. And then at the same time, of course, the food has become softer, and that enables us to have smaller teeth and smaller jaws, a flatter face, and less prognathous jaws. At the same time we, in fact, have smaller guts and a shift in the arrangement of our guts that reflects the fact that we're eating food that is relatively highly digestible. So we have long small intestines, the part of the gut that absorbs the products of digestion, and we have short large intestines where fermentation goes on when you retain food that takes twenty-four hours or more to be fermented under the action of bacteria. We have relatively little food that comes in that needs to be fermented. All of these changes are easily explained by the adoption of cooking.

ET: *How much did our brains and bodies change as a result of eating cooked food?*

RW: The standard estimate is that female bodies increased in weight by about 60 percent around the 1.9-million-year mark. So, if you compare the body size of about 125 pounds for an average woman with the average range of 70 to 80 pounds for a chimp, it's really quite a big increase. And the brain size is going up...it might be 60 percent.

ET: *You've said that cooking and meat eating are the only two proposals for what transformed the ape into a human. Why couldn't the changes just be from eating more raw meat rather than cooking?*

RW: We don't know too much about what it's like to chew raw meat because people don't do it. But chimpanzees are a good model because they have teeth that are just about the same size in relation to their bodies as those of our early ancestors 1.9 million years ago. When we look at chimpanzees eating raw meat, it turns out that they're eating it so slowly that it would just take a tremendous amount of time to rely on eating nothing but raw meat. And that would be a problem.

Think about how many calories our early ancestors would have needed at that stage, estimated at somewhere in the low 2000s. This would take five to six hours a day of simply chewing *without* going out and finding more meat, cutting it up, and looking after your babies and so on. And they would have had to develop some kind of tooth arrangement that was sharp and enabled them to chop it up quickly and swallow it in the manner of a carnivore.

It just seems very unlikely that, at any time since 1.9 million years ago, our ancestors were chewing for half the day, because animals that chew a lot have got deep jaws and robust bones in the mouth to accommodate the stresses of the chewing. That's not what you see—our ancestors' jaws have been built relatively lightly ever since 1.9 million years ago. So, it's not that I think that meat is unimportant; it probably was eaten a lot. It's just that to become important it had to be tenderized to allow it to be eaten easily. The tenderizing could have begun in a physical way by hammering it with stones, maybe, but cooking would have solved the problem much more efficiently.

ET: *When did humans learn how to master fire and then use it for cooking?*

RW: No one knows for sure. But there is such good evidence from caves in southern Europe that humans controlled fire by 400,000 years ago that essentially everyone accepts that fire was controlled by then. So the conservative view is that we started our control of fire then. The 800,000-year date recently published by Goren-Inbar and colleagues in *Science* (April, 2004) is perhaps the best evidence yet for an earlier date for fire. It's particularly nice support for the notion that control of fire must have started before we can see it, because around 800,000 years ago even less happened in human evolution than at 500,000 years ago. People rarely lived in caves before 400,000 years ago, so the remains of earlier campfires can't easily be found. But the more radical view, which seems right to me, is that bits and pieces of archaeological evidence for control of fire at earlier dates, all the way back to 1.9 million years ago, are right. In other words, I believe our species started to control fire at 1.9 million years ago.

Then, the question is, what's the relationship between control of fire and cooking? Some people imagine a period when our ancestors had fire but ate raw food. But, once we had control of fire, I think that we would have started cooking very soon, maybe within a week, maybe within ten generations—but waiting 1,000 or 10,000 or 100,000 years? It's unthinkable. Modern primates, such as monkeys in captivity, allow foods to cook in fires before they take them out. It's obviously just not a big cognitive step from controlling fire to cooking.

So, if humans were cooking by 800,000 years ago, it seems likely that they had been cooking since 1.9 million years ago, because that's when our modern frame evolved. Basically nothing happened in human evolution between 1.9 million years and 800,000 years ago to suggest any improvement in the diet—certainly nothing as radical as being able to shift from raw to cooked food.

ET: *Who was the first cook?*

RW: It was not fully human. It was one of these prehuman hominids around the 2-million-years-ago mark, living somewhere in Africa, perhaps an australopithecine or a species like Homo ergaster [an early form of Homo erectus].

Whenever cooking evolved, we've got this problem of how on earth did the first cook manage to solve the problem of getting to use fire and controlling it rather than running away from it.

One fantasy that I enjoy is the notion that there was something like the chimera that we now see in western Turkey. In western Turkey you've got a mountain, Mount Olympus, where there were several holes in the ground, quite small, just a foot or two across, with fire coming out of them. This fire has been going for at least 2,700 years, judging by the fact that Homer recorded its presence.

To call it permanent fire is too exaggerated, perhaps, but it's said that an earthquake was a cause of some release of gas that's been seeping out ever since then and which has been burning all that time. There are several places around the world where you get little patches of permanent fire burning like this. So it doesn't seem unreasonable to imagine that there was some permanent fire in Africa somewhere.

We know that chimpanzees can learn to be happy with fire. Kanzi is a captive Bonobo (pygmy chimpanzee) who goes for walks with Sue Savage-Rumbaugh in the forests of Georgia (United States). When she asks him to go get firewood and to use matches to light a fire and then to cook up some sausages, he does so. These things are not that difficult for a species as big-brained as a chimpanzee.

So, it's relatively easy to imagine an australopithecine who keeps coming back, sees these flames roaring out of the ground, and starts playing with them. Then it wouldn't be long before they see what happens to one of the roots they have been eating when it is heated by the fire. That may not be the way it happened, but at least it gives a sense of the possibility of the transition. You don't have to be fully human, I think, to imagine that you could tame fire. So, if indeed you were prehuman and started being able to use fire, then that knowledge could be passed on from generation to generation in the many, many years before these species would have actually been able to make fire.

Photo courtesy of shutterstock

ET: *How do you imagine they were cooking?*

RW: The cooking would have been very, very simple. Once you've got a campfire, then it's the way that people cook nowadays. In the bush the main plant food would be roots—African versions of carrots or potatoes often dug from the edge of swamps or lakes. Many would be tough and leathery, pretty nasty in the best of times, but improved enormously by being heated. You'd just rest these on the coals next to the dying flames. After twenty minutes and occasionally turning them, the roots change from something that is extremely fibrous into something that is a lot softer and easier to eat.

Very often the way that people eat meat is they throw a small animal on the flames and that singes the hair off. Then they cut it up. We know that at 1.9 million years they were capable of cutting meat up because there are cut marks [made by stone knives] on fossil animal bones that go back 2.5 million years. So they could have laid strips of meat onto sticks above the fire. Well, maybe it would have taken a little time before that happened. But it doesn't seem very difficult if they had already been cutting up meat for 500,000 years to imagine that they could put small chunks on the embers next to the fire or next to the flames themselves. And all you need to do is heat meat to 170° Fahrenheit, and it reduces enormously the problems that make meat so difficult to eat when it's raw, which is the toughness. Heat coagulates the collagen fibers that make meat tough and turns them brittle. Suddenly, you've got something that you can eat pretty quickly.

ET: *How did humans make the transition from cooking over an outdoor fire to hearths and then to earth ovens?*

RW: No one knows. I imagine that the way things started is that the first kind of controlled fire would be simply sticks on the flat earth. Then at some point you'd start digging a little pit and you might surround it with some stones that would protect it against the wind a little bit further, and maybe other ways I don't know about making the fire more efficient.

An earth oven is a little hole that has been dug in the ground. Hot stones are put into the hole, and the food that you want to cook is put in with those hot stones. Then you stop the hole with earth, and the heat from the stones combined with the moisture of the earth leads to a sort of steaming effect, and you get a rather nice, gentle, slow cooking. That's practiced nowadays in various parts of the world, such as New Guinea and India.

There are other complicated kinds of hearth arrangements in sites in southern Europe, for instance in France in Pech de l'Azé II, that go back 250,000 to 300,000 years. At the entrance you have one kind of hearth arrangement, rings of stones where probably there was some kind of lighting arrangement to scare off predators from coming into the cave. And then inside the cave, in addition to something like an earth oven, there was apparently a cooking area more than a yard across, indicated by flat stones whose red and black colors indicate repeated burning.

But to assume that earth ovens start very quickly seems to me to be an unnecessarily optimistic assumption. Earth ovens look like a pretty complicated kind of technical achievement. I had assumed that this was just a signal that cooking had been going on so long at the point that they had been able to devise various rather ingenious ways of making cooked food even nicer.

ET: *How did cooking affect the social structure?*

RW: I think the social structure is a really interesting question because this is in many ways the biggest gap in the way anybody has thought about cooking so far. Everyone's aware that cooking would have improved the quality of food, so it's not that big a deal to think about it affecting our energy and our teeth and so on. But there's been amazingly little thought given to this question of what cooking did to social structure.

My colleagues and I made the following argument in a paper that we wrote in 1999 that cooking lay at the base of human evolution: The huge problem that cooking presents is that it changes a species from feeding as it picks the food to forcing a species to keep its food for some time, which will be at least twenty minutes to probably several hours during the period when it is gathering it and going to cook it. That means for a period of time there is individual ownership, and once you have ownership, then there is the possibility of competition over those owned goods.

In other words, just as with any other animal where somebody gets a piece of food that is relatively valuable, others will try to pinch it. Female lions bring down the antelope; the male lion comes and takes it away. The low-ranking male chimp kills a monkey; the high-ranking chimp comes and takes it away. The female baboon digs for some roots; the male baboon watches, and just as she reaches to get the results of her labor, he says, "I'll take over, thank you." And in a similar way it seems impossible to imagine that when our ancestors first started cooking there wasn't pressure by which the hungry high-ranking individuals would not have taken advantage of the low-ranking individuals who had done all the hard work to get some meat or dig up the roots and get it cooked. And that problem seems to me to be really severe. We need to think about how we solved it.

ET: *How do you suppose humans solved this problem?*

RW: The human species is the only one, in all of the animals we know, in which there is a thing we call "sexual division of labor." I think it is a slight misnomer because it underestimates the extent to which there is a bias in favor of the male. It implies that the male and female are equal, doing equally well under the sexual division of labor. But women are always the ones that get to do the least favorite tasks, and women are the ones who predictably have to take responsibility for producing a meal in the evening.

Men are free to do what they want. A man can go off every day and hunt for three weeks and never get anything, and still he's going to get food, given to him by his wife in the form of a cooked meal when he returns in the evening. But if a woman goes off and tries to dig for food and never gets anything, she's in big trouble. A man knows that he can rely on a woman to produce food for him; a woman has nobody to rely on, she has to do it for herself.

So a woman is more like a chimpanzee, as it were: she is producing for herself, and then she has the problem of somebody who's taking some food away from her. A man is an entirely new species of animal, because a man is relying on others to feed him every evening. Now it's true that he will often produce foods that he will give to his wife, and the relationship can be beneficial. But some men don't. Some men are lousy producers, and they are still able to take advantage of the system. The problem is not so much why did men and women divide and then cooperate. We should be asking this question instead: "Why it is that men are able to get away without having to be responsible for their own food supply?"

ET: *Why aren't men responsible for their own food supply?*

RW: I put these two observations together: On the one hand, there's the fact that you know that there's going to be pressure to steal the food of low-ranking individuals. On the other hand, there's the fact that only in our species is there a sex that doesn't have to collect their own food every day. Among hunters and gatherers, men are able to get away with not feeding themselves. The solution is that males have developed a relationship with females in which they protect a female's food supply from everybody else in the community. And in exchange, she feeds him.

The way I imagine it working in the past was something like this. Around the ancient campfire you have females getting their own food. Then you find males who are coming back in the evening, having been unsuccessful in hunting or getting any other food. Maybe they were off chasing other women instead of trying to find honey. So now they've got nothing to eat, and they bully a female into giving them some of her food.

And that kind of social pressure creates a situation in which it pays every female to develop a friendly relationship with a male who will protect her from being bullied by a whole herd of males. Better to have one male to protect your food supply and predictably feed him, if he can keep everybody else off, than be a lone female who is exposed to the possibility of theft from many other individuals. The male is an effective protector of her food supply because he's part of a system of respect among males. In a sense, he pays other males to stay away because he's part of a food-getting system in which whenever he does get food, he shares it on a predictably culturally agreed equal basis with other males. So, all the males are in an arrangement whereby they agree not to interfere with each other, and the female is in a relationship with the male whereby he agrees to keep all the other males off. It seems to make sense.

ET: *How has cooking affected human life history—how fast we grow, for instance?*

RW: These are areas that still haven't been well explored. But of course one of the most dramatic things about human life history is the fact that we have children that are dependent. This is different from chimpanzees, for instance, where the infants are weaned at about the three- to five-year stage and then they're independent. The only way chimpanzees feed each other is through nursing.

Whereas with humans, the child is being fed until it's an early adolescent. Children make some contribution to the domestic work and food gathering and so on, but nevertheless, the net flow of energy is definitely from the parent to the child, not just until weaning but all the time until at least 10 to 12 years old. So, childhood (a period of economic dependency beyond weaning) is normally regarded as a special human feature.

And childhood is made possible by cooking, because a species that cooks can easily overproduce. A chimpanzee that spends six hours collecting and chewing her own food doesn't have time to collect extra food to give to her children. But a foraging woman can collect and cook enough food to feed her family. Instead of spending six hours a day eating, she spends only about one hour eating. That leaves enough time to gather and cook for others.

Then, earlier in the life span, for at least 20,000 years, babies have been given cooked mush so they can abandon nursing very early. The result is that the mother has less energetic strain on her body, so she's able to have a relatively quick interbirth interval of three to four years, whereas in chimpanzees it's more like five to six years. That is presumably because even though the women still have children with them, they're able to feed them by cooking and still get enough food themselves to return to a high rate of ovulation.

So, cooking gives us big families—dependent children, produced relatively quickly.

ET: *What effect does cooking have on the human mortality rate?*

RW: Well, it's very interesting that humans have a very low rate of mortality. If you compare humans and chimps, at every age humans are dying more slowly than chimpanzees. This is not because of predation, because most of the chimp populations have not been subject to predation. It's just something inherent about their bodies. The implication is that the immune system or other systems of defense are less effective in chimps than they are in humans. I don't want to suggest that this is well known, but I think it's an interesting speculation. Part of what's happening as humans are able to acquire more energy as a result of cooking and eating superior food may be that they're able to divert a proportion of that energy into the kinds of defenses that enable us to live a long time.

ET: *Are there problems with humans today eating too much or only meat?*

RW: Nowadays, people can eat a tremendous amount of meat because there's a lot of fat to go with it. But if you're eating meat from the wild, which has very little fat and is mostly protein, then there is a problem with getting rid of the urea that is produced by digestion of excess protein. Urea poisoning can result. So too much meat can definitely be bad for you.

Of course, people in rich countries eat too much of everything. Indeed, the irony is that although cooked food has been so important for human evolution, raw food might be one of the healthiest diets for today. A raw-food diet is possible in rich countries today because of our low level of physical activity, the high agricultural quality of foods that go into a modern raw-food diet, and the extensive processing that makes raw foods palatable and easily digested. Even so, it takes a tremendous amount of determination to stick to a raw-food diet, because you'll feel hungry so much of the time. If you can do it, however, you'll bring your caloric intake nicely down, and maybe you'll have the philosophical satisfaction of imagining what the lives of our prehuman ancestors were like in those distant days before cooking was invented.

In his interview, Richard Wrangham locates our evolution from ape to human in cooking and meat eating. Why might some consider this a provocative claim? Which audiences, including those inside scientific and culinary communities, might find this claim controversial?

Wrangham uses a range of evidence—primary and secondary studies, empirical analysis, deductive and inductive reasoning—to convince his audiences of the radical change in the human species with the advent of cooking. As a group, find examples of the different kinds of evidence Wrangham uses. Evaluate the strengths and weaknesses of his proofs. In what contexts might these different types of evidence work best?

Poet, novelist, and essayist Wendell Berry has spent much of his life thinking, writing, and teaching about American life in general, and agricultural life in particular. Berry wrote the following essay in 1989, and as it makes clear, he is an eloquent and determined critic of farm and food policies that continue to move Americans further away from the land—literally and figuratively.

THE PLEASURES OF EATING

By Wendell Berry

Many times, after I have finished a lecture on the decline of American farming and rural life, someone in the audience has asked, "What can city people do?"

"Eat responsibly," I have usually answered. Of course, I have tried to explain what I mean by that, but afterwards I have invariably felt there was more to be said than I had been able to say. Now I would like to attempt a better explanation.

I begin with the proposition that eating is an agricultural act. Eating ends the annual drama of the food economy that begins with planting and birth. Most eaters, however, are no longer aware that this is true. They think of food as an agricultural product, perhaps, but they do not think of themselves as participants in agriculture. They think of themselves as "consumers." If they think beyond that, they recognize that they are passive consumers. They buy what they want—or what they have been persuaded to want—within the limits of what they can get. They pay, mostly without protest, what they are charged. And they mostly ignore certain critical questions about the quality and the cost of what they are sold: How fresh is it? How pure or clean is it, how free of dangerous chemicals? How far was it transported, and what did transportation add to the cost? How much did manufacturing or packaging or advertising add to the cost? When the food product has been manufactured or "processed" or "precooked," how has that affected its quality or price or nutritional value?

Photo by Peter Menzel

The Revis family of North Carolina, with the food they'll consume in a typical month, from the book *Hungry Planet: What the World Eats* by Peter Menzel and Faith D'Aluisio.

Most urban shoppers would tell you that food is produced on farms. But most of them do not know what farms, or what kinds of farms, or where the farms are, or what knowledge of skills are involved in farming. They apparently have little doubt that farms will continue to produce, but they do not know how or over what obstacles. For them, then, food is pretty much an abstract idea—something they do not know or imagine—until it appears on the grocery shelf or on the table.

The specialization of production induces specialization of consumption. Patrons of the entertainment industry, for example, entertain themselves less and less and have become more and more passively dependent on commercial suppliers. This is certainly true also of patrons of the food industry, who have tended more and more to be mere consumers—passive, uncritical, and dependent. Indeed, this sort of consumption may be said to be one of the chief goals of industrial production. The food industrialists have by now persuaded millions of consumers to prefer food that is already prepared. They will grow, deliver, and cook your food for you and (just like your mother) beg you to eat it. That they do not yet offer to insert it, prechewed, into our mouth is only because they have found no profitable way to do so. We may rest assured that they would be glad to find such a way. The ideal industrial food consumer would be strapped to a table with a tube running from the food factory directly into his or her stomach.

Perhaps I exaggerate, but not by much. The industrial eater is, in fact, one who does not know that eating is an agricultural act, who no longer knows or imagines the connections between eating and the land, and who is therefore necessarily passive and uncritical—in short, a victim. When food, in the minds of eaters, is no longer associated with farming and with the land, then the eaters are suffering a kind of cultural amnesia that is misleading and dangerous. The current version of the "dream home" of the future involves "effortless" shopping from a list of available goods on a television monitor and heating precooked food by remote control. Of course, this implies and depends on, a perfect ignorance of the history of the food that is consumed. It requires that the citizenry should give up their hereditary and sensible aversion to buying a pig in a poke. It wishes to make the selling of pigs in pokes an honorable and glamorous activity. The dreams in this dream home will perforce know nothing about the kind or quality of this food, or where it came from, or how it was produced and prepared, or what ingredients, additives, and residues it contains—unless, that is, the dreamer undertakes a close and constant study of the food industry, in which case he or she might as well wake up and play an active and responsible part in the economy of food.

There is, then, a politics of food that, like any politics, involves our freedom. We still (sometimes) remember that we cannot be free if our minds and voices are controlled by someone else. But we have neglected to understand that we cannot be free if our food and its sources are controlled by someone else. The condition of the passive consumer of food is not a democratic condition. One reason to eat responsibly is to live free.

But if there is a food politics, there are also a food esthetics and a food ethics, neither of which is dissociated from politics. Like industrial sex, industrial eating has become a degraded, poor, and paltry thing. Our kitchens and other eating places more and more resemble filling stations, as our homes more and more resemble motels. "Life is not very interesting," we seem to have decided. "Let its satisfactions be minimal, perfunctory, and fast." We hurry through our meals to go to work and hurry through our work in order to "recreate" ourselves in the evenings and on weekends and vacations. And then we hurry, with the greatest possible speed and noise and violence, through our recreation—for what? To eat the billionth hamburger at some fast-food joint, hellbent on increasing the "quality" of our life? And all this is carried out in a remarkable obliviousness to the causes and effects, the possibilities and the purposes, of the life of the body in this world.

One will find this obliviousness represented in virgin purity in the advertisements of the food industry, in which food wears as much makeup as the actors. If one gained one's whole knowledge of food from these advertisements (as some presumably do), one would not know that the various edibles were ever living creatures, or that they all come from the soil, or that they were produced by work. The passive American consumer, sitting down to a meal of pre-prepared or fast food, confronts a platter covered with inert, anonymous substances that have been processed, dyed, breaded, sauced, gravied, ground, pulped, strained, blended, prettified, and sanitized beyond resemblance to any part of any creature that ever lived. The products of nature and agriculture have been made, to all appearances, the products of industry. Both eater and eaten are thus in exile from biological reality. And the result is a kind of solitude, unprecedented in human experience, in which the eater may think of eating as, first, a purely commercial transaction between him and a supplier and then as a purely appetitive transaction between him and his food.

And this peculiar specialization of the act of eating is, again, of obvious benefit to the food industry, which has good reasons to obscure the connection between food and farming. It would not do for the consumer to know that the hamburger she is eating came from a steer who spent much of his life standing deep in his own excrement in a feedlot, helping to pollute the local streams, or that the calf that yielded the veal cutlet on her plate spent its life in a box in which it did not have room to turn around. And, though her sympathy for the slaw might be less tender, she should not be encouraged to meditate on the hygienic and biological implications of mile-square fields of cabbage, for vegetables grown in huge monocultures are dependent on toxic chemicals—just as animals in close confinements are dependent on antibiotics and other drugs.

The consumer, that is to say, must be kept from discovering that, in the food industry—as in any other industry—the overriding concerns are not quality and health, but volume and price. For decades now the entire industrial food economy, from the large farms and feedlots to the chains of supermarkets and fast-food restaurants has been obsessed with volume. It has relentlessly increased scale in order to increase volume in order (probably) to reduce costs. But as scale increases, diversity declines; as diversity declines, so does health; as health declines, the dependence on drugs and chemicals necessarily increases. As capital replaces labor, it does so by substituting machines, drugs, and chemicals for human workers and for the natural health and fertility of the soil. The food is produced by any means or any shortcuts that will increase profits. And the business of the cosmeticians of advertising is to persuade the consumer that food so produced is good, tasty, healthful, and a guarantee of marital fidelity and long life.

It is possible, then, to be liberated from the husbandry and wifery of the old household food economy. But one can be thus liberated only by entering a trap (unless one sees ignorance and helplessness as the signs of privilege, as many people apparently do). The trap is the ideal of industrialism: a walled city surrounded by valves that let merchandise in but no consciousness out. How does one escape this trap? Only voluntarily, the same way that one went in: by restoring one's consciousness of what is involved in eating; by reclaiming responsibility for one's own part in the food economy. One might begin with the illuminating principle of Sir Albert Howard's *The Soil and Health*, that we should understand "the whole problem of health in soil, plant, animal, and man as one great subject." Eaters, that is, must understand that eating takes place inescapably in the world, that it is inescapably an agricultural act, and how we eat determines, to a considerable extent, how the world is used. This is a simple way of describing a relationship that is inexpressibly complex. To eat responsibly is to understand and enact, so far as we can, this complex relationship. What can one do? Here is a list, probably not definitive:

1. Participate in food production to the extent that you can. If you have a yard or even just a porch box or a pot in a sunny window, grow something to eat in it. Make a little compost of your kitchen scraps and use it for fertilizer. Only by growing some food for yourself can you become acquainted with the beautiful energy cycle that revolves from soil to seed to flower to fruit to food to offal to decay, and around again. You will be fully responsible for any food that you grow for yourself, and you will know all about it. You will appreciate it fully, having known it all its life.

2. Prepare your own food. This means reviving in your own mind and life the arts of kitchen and household. This should enable you to eat more

cheaply, and it will give you a measure of "quality control": you will have some reliable knowledge of what has been added to the food you eat.

3. Learn the origins of the food you buy, and buy the food that is produced closest to your home. The idea that every locality should be, as much as possible, the source of its own food makes several kinds of sense. The locally produced food supply is the most secure, freshest, and the easiest for local consumers to know about and to influence.

4. Whenever possible, deal directly with a local farmer, gardener, or orchardist. All the reasons listed for the previous suggestion apply here. In addition, by such dealing you eliminate the whole pack of merchants, transporters, processors, packagers, and advertisers who thrive at the expense of both producers and consumers.

5. Learn, in self-defense, as much as you can of the economy and technology of industrial food production. What is added to the food that is not food, and what do you pay for those additions?

6. Learn what is involved in the best farming and gardening.

7. Learn as much as you can, by direct observation and experience if possible, of the life histories of the food species.

The last suggestion seems particularly important to me. Many people are now as much estranged from the lives of domestic plants and animals (except for flowers and dogs and cats) as they are from the lives of the wild ones. This is regrettable, for these domestic creatures are in diverse ways attractive; there is such pleasure in knowing them. And farming, animal husbandry, horticulture, and gardening, at their best, are complex and comely arts; there is much pleasure in knowing them, too.

It follows that there is great displeasure in knowing about a food economy that degrades and abuses those arts and those plants and animals and the soil from which they come. For anyone who does know something of the modern history of food, eating away from home can be a chore. My own inclination is to eat seafood instead of red meat or poultry when I am traveling. Though I am by no means a vegetarian, I dislike the thought that some animal has been made miserable in order to feed me. If I am going to eat meat, I want it to be from an animal that has lived a pleasant, uncrowded life outdoors, on bountiful pasture, with good water nearby and trees for shade. And I am getting almost as fussy about food plants. I like to eat vegetables and fruits that I know have lived happily and healthily in good soil, not the products of the huge, bechemicaled factory-fields that I have seen, for example, in the Central Valley of California. The industrial farm is said to have been patterned on the factory production line. In practice, it looks more like a concentration camp.

The pleasure of eating should be an extensive pleasure, not that of the mere gourmet. People who know the garden in which their vegetables have grown and know that the garden is healthy and remember the beauty of the growing plants, perhaps in the dewy first light of morning when gardens are at their best. Such a memory involves itself with the food and is one of the pleasures of eating. The knowledge of the good health of the garden relieves and frees and comforts the eater. The same goes for eating meat. The thought of the good pasture and of the calf contentedly grazing flavors the steak. Some, I know, will think of it as bloodthirsty or worse to eat a fellow creature you have known all its life. On the contrary, I think it means that you eat with understanding and with gratitude. A significant part of the pleasure of eating is in one's accurate consciousness of the lives and the world from which food comes. The pleasure of eating, then, may be the best available standard of our health. And this pleasure, I think, is pretty fully available to the urban consumer who will make the necessary effort.

I mentioned earlier the politics, esthetics, and ethics of food. But to speak of the pleasure of eating is to go beyond those categories. Eating with the fullest pleasure—pleasure, that is, that does not depend on ignorance—is perhaps the profoundest enactment of our connection with the world. In this pleasure we experience and celebrate our dependence and our gratitude, for we are living from mystery, from creatures we did not make and powers we cannot comprehend. When I think of the meaning of food, I always remember these lines by the poet William Carlos Williams, which seem to me merely honest:

> There is nothing to eat,
> seek it where you will,
> but the body of the Lord.
> The blessed plants
> and the sea, yield it
> to the imagination intact.

Explore

Berry describes "patrons of the food industry" as "passive, uncritical, and dependent" for their lack of active questioning and involvement in food production. Do you know where your food comes from? Interview one of your food providers—your school's food contractor, the manager or chef at a restaurant that you frequently visit, your grocery's produce or meat manager, or a farmer at a farmers' market—and trace the steps a particular food item goes through to make it to you. Where was the item grown, processed, handled? How was it grown? By whom? How and how far was it transported? What route did your food travel to get to you? When necessary, conduct online research to fill in any gaps.

Invent

Berry's famous line, "eating is an agricultural act," has become a battle cry for farmers and food activists around the world. What does he mean by this? Drawing from your experiences, how else is eating defined? What associations do you have with eating?

Compose

Berry concludes his piece with a list of seven concrete actions readers can take to become more responsible eaters. Revise this list to target a dorm-dwelling, college-aged audience. Think about, for instance, how you might make these suggestions more realistic for a person living in a dorm with little to no kitchen or garden spaces.

Collaborate

Movies like *Food, Inc.* support Berry's suspicion that the food industry "has good reasons to obscure the connection between food and farming." As a class, view *Food, Inc.* and discuss how the stories it tells amplify Berry's argument. Do you think industrial food producers are trying to conceal the way they process food? How do you think (or hope) viewing industrial agricultural practices changes your eating practices?

Using sarcasm and wit to deliver cutting social critiques, David Sedaris has become one of America's most popular humor writers. He wrote "Tasteless" for The New Yorker magazine in 2007. If Wendell Berry describes, in the preceding essay, how we should eat, Sedaris shows us how we should not.

TASTELESS

By David Sedaris

One of the things they promise when you quit smoking is that food will regain its flavor. Taste buds paved beneath decades of tar will spring back to life, and an entire sense will be restored. I thought it would be like putting on a pair of glasses—something dramatic that makes you say, "Whoa!"—but it's been six months now, and I have yet to notice any significant change.

Part of the problem might be me. I've always been in touch with my stomach, but my mouth and I don't really speak. Oh, it chews all right. It helps me form words and holds stuff when my hands are full, but it doesn't do any of these things very well. It's third-rate at best—fifth if you take my teeth into consideration.

Even before I started smoking, I was not a remarkably attentive eater. "Great fried fish," I'd say to my mother, only to discover that I was eating a chicken breast or, just as likely, a veal cutlet. She might as well have done away with names and identified our meals by color: "Golden brown." "Red." "Beige with some pink in it."

I am a shoveller, a quantity man, and I like to keep going until I feel sick. It's how a prisoner might eat, one arm maneuvering the fork and the other encircling the plate like a fence: head lowered close to my food, eyes darting this way and that; even if I don't particularly like it, it's mine, God damn it.

Some of this has to do with coming from a large family. Always afraid that I wouldn't get enough, I'd start worrying about more long before I finished what was in front of me. We'd be at the dinner table, and, convict-like, out of one side of my mouth, I'd whisper to my sister Amy.

"What'll you take for that chicken leg?"

"You mean my barbecued rib?"

"Call it what you like, just give me your asking price."

"Oh gosh," she'd say. "A quarter?"

"Twenty-five cents! What do you think this is—a restaurant?"

She'd raise the baton of meat to her face and examine it for flaws. "A dime."

"A nickel," I'd say, and before she could argue I'd have snatched it away.

I should have been enormous, the size of a panda, but I think that the fear of going without—the anxiety that this produced—acted like a kind of furnace, and burned off the calories before I could gain weight. Even after learning how to make my own meals, I remained, if not skinny, then at least average. My older sister Lisa and I were in elementary school when our mother bought us our first cookbook. The recipes were fairly simple—lots of Jell-O-based desserts and a wheel-shaped meat loaf cooked in an angel-food-cake pan. This last one was miraculous to me. "A meat loaf—with a hole in it!" I kept saying. I guess I thought that as it baked the cavity would fill itself with rubies or butterscotch pudding. How else to explain my disappointment the first dozen times I made it?

In high school, I started cooking pizzas—"from scratch," I liked to say, "the ol' fashioned way." On Saturday afternoons, I'd make my dough, place it in a cloth-covered bowl, and set it in the linen closet to rise. We'd have our dinner at seven or so, and four hours later, just as "Shock Theater," our local horror-movie program, came on, I'd put my pizzas in the oven. It might have been all right if this were just part of my evening, but it was everything: all I knew about being young had canned Parmesan cheese on it. While my classmates were taking acid and having sex in their cars, I was arranging sausage buttons and sliced peppers into smiley faces.

"The next one should look mad," my younger brother would say. And, as proof of my versatility, I would create a frown.

To make it all that much sadder, things never got any better than this. Never again would I take so many chances or feel such giddy confidence in my abilities. This is not to say that I stopped cooking, just that I stopped trying.

Between the year that I left my parents' house and the year that I met Hugh, I made myself dinner just about every night. I generally alternated between three or four simple meals, but if forced to name my signature dish I'd probably have gone with my *Chicken and Linguine with Grease on It*. I don't know that I ever had an actual recipe; rather, like my *Steak and Linguine with Blood on It*, I just sort of played it by ear. The good thing about those meals was that they had only two ingredients. Anything more than that and I'm like Hugh's mother buying Christmas presents. "I look at the list, I go to the store, and then I just freeze," she says.

I suggest that it's nothing to get worked up about, and see in her eyes the look I give when someone says, "It's only a dinner party," or "Can we have something with the Chicken and Linguine with Grease on It?"

I cook for myself when I'm alone; otherwise, Hugh takes care of it, and happily, too. People tell me that he's a real chef, and something about the way they say it, a tone of respect and envy, leads me to believe them. I know that the dinners he prepares are correct. If something is supposed to be hot, it is. If it looks rust-colored in pictures, it looks rust-colored on the plate. I'm always happy to eat Hugh's cooking, but when it comes to truly tasting, to discerning the subtleties I hear others talking about, it's as if my tongue were wearing a mitten.

That's why fine restaurants are wasted on me. I suppose I can appreciate the lighting, or the speed with which my water glass is refilled, but, as far as the food is concerned, if I can't distinguish between a peach and an apricot I really can't tell the difference between an excellent truffle and a mediocre one. Then, too, the more you pay the less they generally give you to eat. French friends visiting the United States are floored by the size of the portions. "Plates the size of hubcaps!" they cry. "No wonder the Americans are so fat."

"I know," I say. "Isn't it awful?" Then I think of Claim Jumper, a California-based chain that serves a massive hamburger called the Widow Maker. I ordered a side of creamed spinach there, and it came in what looked like a mixing bowl. It was like being miniaturized, shrunk to the height of a leprechaun or a doll and dropped in the dining room of regular-sized people. Even the salt and pepper shakers seemed enormous. I ate at Claim Jumper only once, and it was the first time in years that I didn't corral my plate. For starters, my arm wasn't long enough, but even if it had been I wouldn't have felt the need. There was plenty to go around, some of it brown, some of it green, and some a color I've come to think of, almost dreamily, as enough.

Explore

Sedaris uses humor to deflate the self-righteous attitude that sometimes accompanies personal writing about food. Look in your library or online at other food narratives in *The New Yorker*, where this essay first ran. What characteristics and sensibilities define these pieces? Does Sedaris's total lack of food awareness (for instance, his inability to tell the difference between a chicken leg and a barbecued rib) play on your expectations of food narratives? How so?

Compose

Are you a quantity-eater, like Sedaris, or a quality-eater? Write a brief essay in which you describe your most memorable meal. What made it special? What elements, be they ingredients or portion size, made this meal different from your everyday eating experiences?

Jessica B. Harris, a professor at the City University of New York, is the author of 10 cookbooks that document the culture and food of the African diaspora. This memoir was published in Gastropolis: Food and New York City, a 2009 collection about New Yorkers' relationships with food.

THE CULINARY SEASONS OF MY CHILDHOOD

BY JESSICA B. HARRIS

Few culinary traditions are as undocumented as those of middle-class African Americans. Scroll back to the 1950s, when segregation was still rampant in the South, and the foodways are even less well known. Although they are briefly mentioned in a few autobiographical narratives and in some fiction, the concern of most African Americans was more with throwing off the shackles of southern segregations that our forebears had come north to escape. This is reflected in our life tales more than in our recollections of meals eaten and foods purchased. The result is that most outsiders believe that ham hocks and hard times are the only remnants of our culinary past. Certainly there were plenty of ham hocks and no shortage of hard times. In fact, my New Jersey-born and raised mother always claimed that that state could best Mississippi in the racist sweepstakes and that she had the stories to prove it! In North and South alike, middle-class African Americans ate the same cornbread and fried chicken and chitterlings and foods from the traditions of the African diaspora as did our less well-off counterparts, but we also ate differently, foods that expressed our middle classness and reflected our social and political aspirations.

Even though chitterlings might be on the menu, they could equally likely be accompanied by a mason jar of corn liquor or a crystal goblet of champagne. Southern specialties like fried porgies and collard greens show up for dinner, but they might be served along with dishes becoming common in an increasingly omnivorous United States that was just beginning its love affair with food.

Nowhere is this more evident than in my own life and in the culinary season of my childhood.

A descendant of the enslaved and free Africans who made their way north in the Great Migration, I grew up in a transplanted southern culture that still remains a vibrant region of the African American culinary world. My family, like many others long separated from the South, raised me in ways that continued their eating traditions, so now I can head south and sop biscuits in gravy, suck chewy bits of fat from a pig's foot spattered with hot sauce, and yes'm and no'm with the best of 'em.

But that's not all of me. I also am a postwar baby who was the only child of striving middle-class parents who were old enough to have been young African American adults in the poverty of the Great Depression. They showered me with love and childhood coddling that makes my childhood seem like an African American version of *The Little Princess*. I also am a child at the confluence of two major African American culinary traditions. My mother's family could claim a smidge of black southern aristocracy, as they were descended from free people of color who migrated to Roanoke, Virginia. My father's family was from Tennessee and had upcountry Georgia roots that extended down the Natchez Trace. Both families showed their backgrounds at the table.

My maternal grandmother, Bertha Philpot Jones, was the quintessential African American matriarch presiding over a groaning board filled with savory goods. The role has become a visual cliché in movies like *The Nutty Professor Part II: The Klumps, Soul Food*, and *Dear Departed*, which revel in the dysfunction of African American life. No such dysfunction, however, was tolerated at Grandma Jones's table; she would not allow it. She was the matriarch and absolute sovereign of the Jones family; she ruled with a delicate but steel-boned hand, and the family marched to her tune. Watermelon-rind pickles spiced with fragrant cinnamon and whole cloves and the reassuring warmth of a full oven wafting smells of roasted joints and freshly baked bread are the aromas I most associate with her. She was a Baptist minister's wife and could put a hurtin' on some food. She had to, for as the minister's wife, she had not only her own brood of twelve children plus husband to feed, but the church folks who dropped in to take care of as well. She pickled fruits like Seckel pears, which had a curiously tart-sweet taste that comes back to me even today. The smell of Parker House rolls, the warmth of the kitchen, and the closeness of a large family all were part of the thrill of Grandma Jones's house. I didn't see her often – only on holidays and special occasions when we'd take the Holland Tunnel to head off to Plainfield, New Jersey, to visit and sit around the table.

Ida Irene Harris, my paternal grandmother, was at the other end of the culinary spectrum. I saw her much more often, at least once a week. When I travel in the South, folks are astounded to hear that as a child I had no southern roots, no grandmother to visit by segregated train or bus under the tutelage of kindly porters and with a tag pinned to my coat. Instead, my South was in the North, for Grandma Harris, in her day-to-day existence, re-created the preserved-in-amber South of her nineteenth-century rural youth in the precincts of her small apartment in the South Jamaica projects. I remember her apartment well, particularly the kitchen, with the four-burner stove on which she made lye soap, the refrigerator that always contained a pitcher of grape Kool-Aid with lemons cut up in it, and the sink in which she washed clothes, punching them with a broomstick to make sure they would get clean. Most of all, I remember the taste of the collard greens that she prepared: verdant, lush with just enough smoked pig parts and fat for seasoning; they were the culinary embodiment of her love and, along with her silky beaten biscuits, one of the few dishes that she made well.

Grandma Harris lived in a self-created southern world. For years, she maintained a small garden plot at the back of the South Jamaica projects. This was just after the victory gardens of World War II when tenants could plant a small plot of land if they wished. Grandma Harris grew southern staples: collard and mustard greens, peanuts, snap beans, and more. I remember her weeding the peanuts and breaking off a leaf of the greens to test for ripening as the Long Island Rail Road train roared by on the tracks above. She taught me to love the slip of boiled peanuts, to sop biscuits in Alaga syrup with butter cut up in it, and to savor the tart sourness of buttermilk long before there was any romance to things southern.

I didn't understand the education she'd given me until years later, in Senegal's Theatre Daniel Sorano, I heard a griot sing. It was as though Grandma Harris had leaned down from the clouds and touched me. The timbre, the tone, the almost keening wail of the Mandinka singer captured the tuneless songs that Grandma sang as she went about her daily tasks, as much as the tastes of the Senegalese food recalled flavors from my childhood. It was then that I realized that unknown to both of us, Grandma Harris had taught me the ways of the past in her demeanor, her stalwartness, her faith, and her food. Those ways would help me survive. She also taught me to behave. I will never forget the summer day when she administered the only childhood whipping I can recall.

"Whipping" was not a word that was used in my house as I was growing up. I was a Dr. Spock baby through and through, and discipline was more about firm conversation than about Daddy's belt. At Grandma Harris's apartment, though, the rules changed and that one time, I knew I was going to get a whipping for sure.

Grandma Harris was another kind of old-line southern matriarch. It didn't matter that she lived on the third floor of the South Jamaica projects in Queens; her world was deeply rooted in the traditions of her South. She would brook no contradiction about manners. In her home, New Year's was celebrated with a mix of collard, mustard, and turnip greens that she had stewed down to a low gravy to accompany the obligatory hoppin' John and chitterlings. I always passed on the chitterlings and ate the hoppin' John, but the greens were my favorite. I had even more respect for them after they caused my downfall and earned me my only childhood whipping.

It happened on a summer's day when I was about six or seven. My mother worked, so I was sent to Grandma's apartment to spend the day in the traditional, extended-family day-care arrangement. I spent most of those urban summer days of my early childhood in her small one-bedroom apartment reading in a chair and staying out from under her feet in order to avoid going outside to play with the other kids, who invariably made fun of my private-school vowels and bookish ways. She, on the other side, spent her days insisting that I go out and play with the "nice children" who all called her Mother Harris.

On the day in question, when I had managed to avoid the dreaded piss-smelling barrels and rough boys and girls of the playground, she looked up from her sewing and said, "Jessica, come here." I was in for it. I was pleasantly surprised when, instead of ordering me downstairs, she instead went for her purse and gave me some money wrapped in a hankie with instructions to go to Miranda's, the Italian-owned corner market, and get a piece of "streak-a-lean-streak-a-fat" for the greens that she was going to cook.

Thrilled at being sent on an errand and overjoyed at escaping the barrel torture, I headed off. The walk was short, only a scant block through the maze of red-brick buildings that had not yet deteriorated into the breeding ground of hopelessness they were to become. A few small trees were in leaf, and the sounds of other children playing reminded me how grown up I was. *I was on an errand.* Arriving at Miranda's, I went directly to the meat counter, where, as in most African American neighborhoods, there was a vast array of pig parts both identifiable and unknown. Having not a clue about streak-a-lean-streak-a-fat but feeling exceptionally sophisticated in my seven-year-old head, I pointed to the slab bacon that my mother used to season things and asked for the requisite amount. It was brought out for my examination, and I grandly pronounced it fine. Cut off to the desired thickness and wrapped in slick brown paper, it was presented to me with solemnity. I tucked it into the net shopping bag that Grandma had provided and headed back home, proud and pleased.

I pushed open the heavy downstairs door and ran up the concrete steps, heels clanking on the metal treads that lined them. When I got to 3B, I pushed through the door that Grandma always kept open in those kinder times and headed in to present my parcel. To my amazement, when she opened it, she began to mutter and ask me what I had gotten.

"Streak-a-lean-streak-a-fat," I replied.

"Did you ask for it?" she questioned.

"No, I pointed it out to the man," I ventured with increasing timidity.

"Well, this isn't it! I wanted what I asked for, streak-a-lean-streak-a-fat," she countered. "This is slab bacon!"

"It's the same thing, isn't it?" I queried.

"NO! Now you march right back there and get me what I asked for, streak-a-lean-streak-a-fat. Take this back!"

"But?"

"No Buts! Just march back there, young lady! Right Now!"

I trudged back to Miranda's, each step made heavier with the thought of having to tell the butcher that I'd made an error and hoping that he'd take back the offending bacon. The joy of escape of the prior hour had soured into a longing for the nasty boys and the stinky barrels. Luckily, the man took pity on bourgie old me and took back the bacon, replacing it with a fattier piece of streaky pork that was a fraction of the price.

When I got back to the building, Grandma was sitting on the benches out front and waiting for me. She uttered the five words that I'd never heard her say: "Go cut me a switch."

Terrified, I set off and hunted for the smallest branch that I could find in this virtually treeless urban landscape, knowing what was coming next. I returned with a smallish green switch that I had unearthed lord knows where. She took a few halfhearted passes at my legs, solemnly repeating with each one, "Don't think you're smarter than your elders." Tears flowed on both sides: mine because I'd certainly learned my lesson through the humiliation of returning the bacon followed by the public whipping, Grandma's because she adored me and wanted a respectful granddaughter. Despite that childhood trauma, I still love collard greens and never eat my New Year's mess of them without remembering Grandma Harris. I always season them with what I have come to think of as streak-a-lean-streak-a-fat-cut-me-a-switch; savor their smoky, oily splendor; and think of the southern lessons she taught me with every bite.

The other days of my early summers were spent with my working parents. We left New York City for family vacations, and I can remember the ice man delivering big blocks of ice wrapped in burlap to chill the icebox of the small cabin that we rented on Three Mile Harbor Road in East Hampton long before the area attained its current vogue. The year after my whipping, when I was eight, we visited Oak Bluffs, Massachusetts, the African American summer community on Martha's Vineyard that has become much touted these days. It was love at first sight, and my parents bought a summer house there that winter.

From the time I was nine until the present, this house has been a part of every summer. Then we made long trips on the Boston Post Road and the Merritt Parkway up to the Wood's Hole ferry dock. Old habits die hard, and my parents in the 1950s would no more think of hitting the road without a shoebox full of fried chicken, deviled eggs, pound cake, oranges, and raisins and a thermos full of lemonade or some other cool drink than they would leave home without maps and a tank full of gas.

Oak Bluffs was just beginning to grow in popularity among New Yorkers; Bostonians knew about its glories long before we did. Middle-class African Americans from New York and New Jersey summered in Sag Harbor near the Hamptons, but my prescient father did not want to be so close to the city that friends could drop in unannounced on the weekends, so it was Martha's Vineyard for us. We joked that if we lost our way to the Vineyard, we could simply follow the trail of chicken bones left by fellow black New Yorkers and find the ferry pier with no problem. Like us, they were marked by segregated back doors and the lack of on-the-road facilities and also stuck to the old ways. We brought our chicken along for years until the Connecticut Turnpike was completed, and then we gradually left the chicken and deviled eggs at home and settled for the mediocre fare of the rest stops. I was thrilled several years ago when a friend, Alexander Smalls, opened a restaurant in Grand Central Terminal celebrating our traveling ways; it was called the Shoebox Café. While the menu was his own inventive interpretation of the black food of the South, I knew he was also honoring the past that many black Americans share.

My Vineyard summers were where I caught my first fish, a porgy of respectable size, and learned to strip the skin off an eel and find out just how delicious the sweet meat was, once you got over the snake look, and to pick mussels off the docks at Menemsha. The days were punctuated by sharing meals with family and friends, waiting for my father to appear on the Friday night "daddy boat" to spend the weekends, and savoring rainy days because my mother treated us with one of her fantastic blueberry cobblers prepared with berries we had picked before the storm came, from the bushes that grew wild along the roadsides. July folded into August marked by county fairs, cotton candy, Illumination Night, Darling's molasses puff, swordfish at Giordano's restaurant, and movies at the Strand or Islander movie houses, accompanied by hot buttered popcorn served from a copper kettle. Soon it was time to pack the car again and head back to our house in Queens. I never really minded because autumn brought the return to school, and my world expanded one hundredfold. My school saw to that.

The United Nations International School was and is a special place. As the first non-UN-connected child to attend the school and one of very few Americans enrolled in the early years, my playmates were the world. UNIS, as the school is called by the cognoscenti, was small, then so small that it added a grade each year until it finally stretched from prekindergarten through high school. Inside Queens's Parkway Village apartments that had been transformed into classrooms, I made lifelong friends and learned how to function in a world that extended to the globe's four corners. A trip to Vasu's or Shikha's house brought smells of the Indian subcontinent, and on occasions when I was fortunate enough to be invited to birthday parties, there were tastes of rich spices and heady unknown flavors that would never have turned up on the table of my garlic-free household. The rich stews of central Europe were featured at Danuta's, and steak and kidney pie might turn up on the table at Eluned's. I can still feel the rasp of the embossed silver spoon-backs that were used on the table at Jennifer and Susan's house in Great Neck and remember their mother's wonderful way with shortbread with nostalgia that can still make my mouth water more than forty-five years later. The annual round of birthday parties was interrupted by school events like international potluck suppers. Parents brought dishes from around the globe, and students began culinary competitions like eating spaghetti with chopsticks in the days before Asian noodle bowls and the vast array of Italian pastas became common culinary currency.

As more Americans joined the school community, even they displayed amazing culinary inventiveness, and I remember being invited to a formal Coke-tail party at Anne's house, where we were served all manner of multihued nonalcoholic cocktails in delicate stemmed glassware complete with swizzle sticks, umbrella garnishes, and lots of maraschino cherries at a birthday fête that was every young girl's dream. All the class events seemed to center on international households of like-acting folk who proved to me at an early age that no matter what turned up on the table, it was to be savored and eaten with gusto.

During the twelve or so years that I attended UNIS, I grew to understand something about the world's food. My core group of friends spent many of those years together, and we became familiar with one another's households and foods and, with that growing knowledge, came to realize that the table was not only where we held our parties and our class fêtes but also where we worked out our problems and got answers to questions about one another. With hindsight, I now realize that we achieved at our birthday tables and communal suppers the same détente and understanding that the parents of many of my friends worked so hard to attain at the tables at which they tried to bring peace to the world.

If my grandmothers' tables gave me a grounding in the African American past that is so much the bedrock of all that I do, and UNIS gave me an understanding of the food of the world, a palate that is open to tasting just about anything, and the knowledge that more friends are made around the table than just about anywhere else, my parents and our daily life completed the picture with the finishing touches.

I have saved my household for last, for it, more than any of the other outside influences, marked the season of my childhood eating. While I grew up at the confluence of two African American culinary traditions and lived in an international world at school, at home on Anderson Road in St. Albans, Queens, my surroundings were a wondrous combination of my parents' dueling culinary wills.

Very few African Americans are to the manor born; most of us have a past of want or need, if not for love, then for cash and the opportunities it can bring. My father, Jesse Brown Harris, was such a person. He was a black man and a striking one at that, aubergine-hued with the carriage of an emperor of Songhai. Early photos show him tall and slender, looking very proprietary about his little family of three. Daddy was not a numbers runner. Daddy was not a welfare ducker or an absentee father. Daddy was just Daddy, and the constancy of that statement and my lack of awareness that this was not the norm for all black children made me different.

As a teenager, Daddy had lived over the stables and worked as a Shabbas goy in Williamsburg, Brooklyn. Until the day he died, he was marked by a childhood of grinding poverty during which he had worn flour-bag suits to school and church, cadged coal at the railroad yard for heat, and picked dandelion leaves on the Fisk College campus for dinner. He was torn between the desire to overcome his past and provide differently for his family and the need to remember it with honor.

My father ate southern food whenever he could cajole my mother into preparing the hog maws or chitterlings that he adored. We even put a stove into the basement of our house so that the smell would not taint our living quarters. He would occasionally bring home cartons of buttermilk, which he would savor with squares of the flaky and hot cornbread that my mother baked at the drop of a hat. Sunday breakfast was his special time, and he would proudly sit at the head of the table and sop up his preferred mix of Karo dark with butter cut up in it with the hoecake that was off-limits to anyone else in the household.

He was the only one in his family of man children who did not and could not cook. My Uncle Bill, his older brother, gave me my first taste of rabbit stew, and my Uncle Jim's spaghetti sauce was the stuff of family legend. Actually, my father cared little for food, but he loved restaurants and, with his increasing affluence, dined out with the best of them. In the early years, dining out meant heading to the local silver bullet diner near our house for specials like mashed potatoes with gravy and Salisbury steak or sauerbraten (the neighborhood was German before we moved in). The bakery on Linden Boulevard, the main shopping street, sold flaky butter cookies and gingerbread at Christmas. Later, when St. Albans became blacker, we would head to Sister's Southern Diner after church on Sundays, still dressed in our Sabbath finery, for down-home feasts of smothered pork chops and greens or stewed okra and fried fish in an orgy of southern feasting that Mommy did not have to cook. In later years, restaurants like the Brasserie, La Fonda del Sol, and the Four Seasons were where we celebrated birthdays and anniversaries. There, my father's duality surfaced, and he would order wine for the bucket or "spittoon," as we had baptized it in our family jargon, and crepes suzette or Caesar salad for the flamboyant tableside service, but we three secretly knew that all the while what he really wanted was a ham hock and some butterbeans to satisfy the tastes of his youth.

My mother, though, truly loved food and had amazing taste buds that could analyze the components of a dish with startling accuracy. She would then reproduce her version of it at home, to the delight of all. Trained as a dietician, my mother reveled in entertaining and entranced her friends with her culinary inventiveness. Decades later, she revealed that at school, she had been required to sit through classes on how to keep black people out of restaurants and was discouraged from doing anything with food demonstrations that would put her in public view. After a brief stint as a dietitian at Bennett College in North Carolina and an even briefer stay in domestic service as a private dietitian, she found that she did not enjoy the field. Instead, she put her talents to use at the supper table, and I grew up eating homemade applesauce and tea sandwiches of olives and cream cheese when my friends were chowing down Gerber's finest and processed cheese spread. Weeknights featured balanced meals like breaded veal cutlets with carrots and peas and a salad, alternating with sublime fried chicken and mashed potatoes or rice and always a green vegetable and salad, or string beans, potatoes, and ham ends slow-cooked into what we called a New England boiled dinner.

Parties were the occasion for pulling out all the stops. My mother would prepare ribbon and pinwheel sandwiches from whole wheat bread, cream cheese, white bread, and strips of red and green bell pepper, long before the spectrum opened up to admit such hues as orange, purple, white, and even yellow! She created cabarets in the basement—persuading her friends to come as babies or in nightclothes, hiring calypso singers, serving drinks with small umbrellas, and devising smoking centerpieces with dry ice and punch bowls—and, each Sunday, presided over tables overflowing with roasts and a multiplicity of vegetables.

My mother created magic in the kitchen and made cooking exciting and fun, with a trick for every dish and a sense of adventure at the stove. As her only child, I got the benefit of this knowledge and accompanied her in the kitchen almost from my birth. In later years, she began to tire of the kitchen, but eventually, she renewed her interest in things culinary and discovered the wonder of ingredients like confit of duck, fresh garlic, pimentos, and arugula. Ever curious, her life was a constant adventure. I did not learn to cook; I simply absorbed it in her kitchen, moving from high chair to small tasks to whole dishes and entire meals.

I am very much the product of all of this, and these seasons of my personal and yet very New York childhood gave me the foods of the world on my plate. For the first years of my life, my fork ranged throughout the world from the simple country food of Grandma Harris to the more elegant Virginia repasts of Grandma Jones and the dishes of the 1950s and 1960s that were, for me, the tastes of home. I also sampled fare from the globe's four corners at the homes of my international classmates and learned that no matter where our origins or our regionalisms, when we eat together and share the commensalism of the table, we make ourselves and our worlds better. It has been said that we are what we eat. I certainly am, and in the many seasons of my New York youth, that included an amazing amount of mighty good food.

Late in her essay, Harris writes: "My core group of friends...became familiar with one another's households and foods and, with that growing knowledge, came to realize that the table was not only where we worked out our problems and got answers to questions about one another." Develop a brief memoir essay in which you explore how food and the experience of preparing or sharing a meal provided more to you than simple sustenance.

Working with a group, discuss how Harris uses her family history to reject and correct common stereotypes about foods that African Americans eat. How does she use food to weave together the various threads of her family background? Be prepared to share your responses with the rest of your class.

According to juliepowellbooks.com: "After a misspent youth involving loads of dead-end jobs and several question-able decisions, Julie Powell, author of Julie & Julia—made into a major motion picture by Nora Ephron starring Meryl Streep and Amy Adams—has found her calling as a writer-cum-butcher. She lives in Long Island City, Queens, when she isn't in Kingston, N.Y., cutting up animals." The following excerpt is the first chapter of Julie & Julia, which itself began as a blog for the online magazine Salon.

DAY 1, RECIPE 1

BY JULIE POWELL

Thursday, October 6, 1949
Paris

At seven o'clock on a dreary evening in the Left Bank, Julia began roasting pigeons for the second time in her life.

She'd roasted them the first time that morning during her first-ever cooking lesson, in a cramped basement kitchen at the Cordon Bleu cooking school at 129, rue du Faubourg St.-Honoré. Now she was roasting some more in the rented flat she shared with her husband, Paul, in the kitchen at the top of a narrow stairway in what used to be the servant quarters before the old house got divided up into apartments. The stove and counters were too short for her, like everything else in the world. Even so, she liked her kitchen at the top of the stairs better than the one at school—liked the light and air up there, liked the dumbwaiter that would carry her birds down to the dining room, liked that she could cook while her husband sat beside her at the kitchen table, keeping her company. She supposed she would get used to the counters soon enough—when you go through life as a six-foot-two-inch-tall woman, you get used to getting used to things.

Paul was there now, snapping pictures of his wife from time to time, and finishing up a letter to his brother, Charlie. "If you could see Julie stuffing pepper and lard up the asshole of a dead pigeon," he wrote, "you'd realize how profoundly affected she's been already."[1]

1 Excerpted from a letter from Paul Child to his brother, Charles, 1949.

But he hadn't seen anything yet. His wife, Julia Child, had decided to learn to cook. She was thirty-seven years old.

THE ROAD TO HELL IS PAVED WITH LEEKS AND POTATOES

As far as I know, the only evidence supporting the theory that Julia Child first made Potage Parmentier during a bad bout of ennui is her own recipe for it. She writes that Potage Parmentier—which is just a Frenchie way of saying potato soup—"smells good, tastes good, and is simplicity itself to make." It is the first recipe in the first book she ever wrote. She concedes that you can add carrots or broccoli or green beans if you want, but that seems beside the point, if what you're looking for is simplicity itself.

Simplicity itself. It sounds like poetry, doesn't it? It sounds like just what the doctor ordered.

It wasn't what my doctor ordered, though. My doctor—my gynecologist, to be specific—ordered a baby.

"There are the hormonal issues in your case, with the PCOS, you know about that already. And you are pushing thirty, after all. Look at it this way—there will never be a better time."

This was not the first time I'd heard this. It had been happening for a couple of years now, ever since I'd sold some of my eggs for $7,500 in order to pay off

Julie Powell (far left) and Julia Child.

credit card debt. Actually, that was the second time I'd "donated"—a funny way of putting it, since when you wake up from the anesthesia less a few dozen ova and get dressed, there's a check for thousands of dollars with *your* name on it waiting at the receptionist's desk. The first time was five years ago, when I was twenty-four, impecunious and fancy-free. I hadn't planned on doing it twice, but three years later I got a call from a doctor with an unidentifiable European accent who asked me if I'd be interested in flying down to Florida for a second go-round, because "our clients were very satisfied with the results of your initial donation." Egg donation is still a new-enough technology that our slowly evolving legal and etiquette systems have not yet quite caught up; nobody knows if egg donators are going to be getting sued for child support ten years down the line or what. So discussions on the subject tend to be knotted with imprecise pronouns and euphemisms. The upshot of this phone call, though, was that there was a little me running around Tampa or somewhere, and the little me's parents were happy enough with him or her that they wanted a matched set. The honest part of me wanted to shout, "Wait, no—when they start hitting puberty you'll regret this!" But $7,500 is a lot of money.

Anyway, it was not until the second harvesting (they actually call it "harvesting"; fertility clinics, it turns out, use a lot of vaguely apocalyptic terms) that I found out I had polycystic ovarian syndrome, which sounds absolutely terrifying, but apparently just meant that I was going to get hairy and fat and I'd have to take all kinds of drugs to conceive. Which means, I guess, that I haven't heard my last of crypto-religious obstetric jargon.

So. Ever since I was diagnosed with this PCOS, two years ago, doctors have been obsessing over my childbearing prospects. I've even been given the Pushing Thirty speech by my avuncular, white-haired *orthopedist* (what kind of twenty-nine-year-old has a herniated disk, I ask you?).

At least my gynecologist had some kind of business in my private parts. Maybe that's why I heroically did not start bawling immediately when he said this, as he was wiping off his speculum. Once he left, however, I did fling one of my navy faille pumps at the place where his head had been just a moment before. The heel hit the door with a thud, leaving a black scuff mark, then dropped onto the counter, where it knocked over a glass jar of cotton swabs. I scooped up all the Q-tips from the counter and the floor and started to stuff them back into the jar before realizing I'd probably gotten them all contaminated, so then I shoved them into a pile next to an apothecary jar full of fresh needles and squeezed myself back into the vintage forties suit I'd been so proud of that morning when Nate from work told me it made my waist look small while subtly eyeing my cleavage, but which on the ride from lower Manhattan to the Upper East Side on an un-air-conditioned 6 train had gotten sweatstained and rumpled. Then I slunk out of the room, fifteen-buck co-pay already in hand, the better to make my escape before anyone discovered I'd trashed the place.

As soon as I got belowground, I knew there was a problem. Even before I reached the turnstiles, I heard a low, subterranean rumble echoing off the tiled walls, and noticed more than the usual number of aimless-looking people milling about. A tangy whiff of disgruntlement wafted on the fetid air. Every once in a great while the "announcement system" would come on and "announce" something, but none of these spatterings of word salad resulted in the arrival of a train, not for a long, long time. Along with everyone else, I leaned out over the platform edge, hoping to see the pale yellow of a train's headlight glinting off the track, but the tunnel was black. I smelled like a rained-upon, nervous sheep. My feet, in their navy heels with the bows on the toe, were killing me, as was my back, and the platform was so crammed with people that before long I began to worry someone was going to fall off the edge onto the tracks—possibly me, or maybe the person I was going to push during my imminent psychotic break.

But then, magically, the crowd veered away. For a split second I thought the stink coming off my suit had reached a deadly new level, but the wary, amused looks on the faces of those edging away weren't focused on me. I followed their gaze to a plug of a woman, her head of salt-and-pepper hair shorn into the sort of crew cut they give to the mentally disabled, who had plopped down on the concrete directly behind me. I could see the whorls of her cowlick like a fingerprint, feel the tingle of invaded personal space against my shins. The woman was muttering to herself fiercely. Commuters had vacated a swath of platform all around the loon as instinctively as a herd of wildebeests evading a lioness. I was the only one stuck in the dangerous blank circle, the lost calf, the old worn-out cripple who couldn't keep up.

The loon started smacking her forehead with the heel of her palm. "Fuck!" she yelled. "Fuck! FUCK!"

I couldn't decide whether it would be safer to edge back into the crowd or freeze where I was. My breathing grew shallow as I turned my eyes blankly out across the tracks to the uptown platform, that old subway chameleon trick.

The loon placed both palms down on the concrete in front of her and—CRACK!—smacked her forehead hard on the ground.

This was a little much even for the surrounding crowd of New Yorkers, who of course all knew that loons and subways go together like peanut butter and chocolate. The sickening noise of skull on concrete seemed to echo in the damp air—as if she was using her specially evolved resonant brainpan as an instrument to call the crazies out from every far-underground branch of the city. Everybody flinched, glancing around nervously. With a squeak I hopped back into the multitude. The loon had a smudgy black abrasion right in the middle of her forehead, like the scuff mark my shoe had left on my gynecologist's door, but she just kept screeching. The train pulled in, and I connived to wiggle into the car the loon wasn't going into.

It was only once I was in the car, squeezed in shoulder to shoulder, the lot of us hanging by one hand from the overhead bar like slaughtered cows on the trundling train, that it came to me—as if some omnipotent God of City Dwellers were whispering the truth in my ear—that the only two reasons I hadn't joined right in with the loon with the gray crew cut, beating my head and screaming "Fuck!" in primal syncopation, were (1) I'd be embarrassed and (2) I didn't want to get my cute vintage suit any dirtier than it already was. Performance anxiety and a dry-cleaning bill; those were the only things keeping me from stark raving lunacy.

That's when I started to cry. When a tear dropped onto the pages of the *New York Post* that the guy sitting beneath me was reading, he just blew air noisily through his nose and turned to the sports pages.

When I got off the subway, after what seemed like years, I called Eric from a pay phone at the corner of Bay Ridge and Fourth Avenue.

"Hey. Did you get anything for dinner?"

Eric made that little sucking-in-through-his-teeth sound he always makes when he thinks he's about to get in trouble. "Was I supposed to?"

"Well, I *told* you I'd be late because of my doctor's appointment—"

"Right, right, sorry. I just, I didn't . . . You want me to order something in, or—"

"Don't worry about it. I'll pick up something or other."

"But I'm going to start packing just as soon as the *NewsHour*'s done, promise!"

It was nearly eight o'clock, and the only market open in Bay Ridge was the Korean deli on the corner of Seventieth and Third. I must have looked a sight, standing around in the produce aisle in my bedraggled suit, my face tracked with mascara, staring like a catatonic. I couldn't think of a thing that I wanted to eat. I grabbed some potatoes, a bunch of leeks, some Hotel Bar butter. I felt dazed and somehow will-less, as if I was following a shopping list someone else had made. I paid, walked out of the shop, and headed for the bus stop, but just missed the B69. There wouldn't be another for a half hour at least, at this time of night, so I started the ten-block walk home, carrying a plastic bag bristling with spiky dark leek bouquets.

It wasn't until almost fifteen minutes later, as I was walking past the Catholic boys' school on Shore Road one block over from our apartment building, that I realized that I'd managed, unconsciously, to buy exactly the ingredients for Julia Child's Potage Parmentier.

When I was a kid, my dad used to love to tell me the story about finding five-year-old Julie curled up in the back of his copper-colored Datsun ZX immersed in a crumpled back issue of the *Atlantic Monthly*. He told that one to all the guys at his office, and to the friends he and my mom went out to dinner with, and to all of the family who weren't born again and likely to disapprove. (Of the *Atlantic*, not Z-cars.)

I think the point behind this was that I'd been singled out as an early entrant to the ranks of the intellectually superior. And since I was awful at ballet and tap dancing, after all, always the last one to make it up the rope in gym class, a girl neither waifish nor charming in owlish red-rimmed glasses, I took my ego-petting where I could get it. But the not-very-highbrow truth of the matter was that the reading was how I got my ya-yas out.

For the sake of my bookish reputation I upgraded to Tolstoy and Steinbeck before I understood them, but my dark secret was that really, I preferred the junk. *The Dragonriders of Pern, Flowers in the Attic, The Clan of the Cave Bear.* This stuff was like my stash of *Playboys* under the mattress. I waited until my camp counselor left the cabin to steal the V.C. Andrews she stashed behind her box of Tampax. I nicked my mom's Jean Auel, and had already gotten halfway through before she found out, so she could only wince and suppose there was some educational value, but no *Valley of Horses* for you, young lady.

Then adolescence set in well and proper, and reading for kicks got shoved in the backseat with the old *Atlantics*. It had been a long time since I'd done anything with the delicious, licentious cluelessness that I used to read those books—hell, sex now wasn't as exciting as reading about sex used to be. I guess nowadays your average fourteen-year-old Texan possesses exhaustive knowledge of the sexual uses of tongue studs, but I doubt the information excites her any more than my revelations about Neanderthal sex.

You know what a fourteen-year-old Texan doesn't know shit about? French food.

A couple of weeks after my twenty-ninth birthday, in the spring of 2002, I went back to Texas to visit my parents. Actually, Eric kind of made me go.

"You have to get out of here," he said. The kitchen drawer that broke two weeks after we moved in, and was never satisfactorily rehabilitated, had just careened off its tracks yet again, flinging Pottery Barn silverware in all directions. I was sobbing, forks and knives glittering at my feet. Eric was holding me in one of those tight hugs like a half nelson, which he does whenever he's trying to comfort me when what he really wants to do is smack me.

"Will you come with me?" I didn't look up from the snot stain I was impressing upon his shirt.

"I'm too busy at the office right now. Besides, I think it's better if you go by yourself. Hang out with your mom. Buy some clothes. Sleep in."

"I have work, though."

"Julie, you're a temp. What's temping for if you can't run off and take a break sometimes? That's why you're doing it, right?"

I didn't like to think about why I was temping. My voice went high and cracked. "Well, I can't afford it."

"We *can* afford it. Or we can ask your parents to pay." He grabbed my chin and lifted it up to his face. "Julie. Seriously? Go. Because I can't live with you like this anymore."

So I went—my mom bought me the ticket for a late birthday present. A week later I flew into Austin, early enough to grab lunch at Poke-Jo's.

And then, right in the middle of my brisket sandwich and okra, less than a month after I turned twenty-nine, Mom dropped the Pushing Thirty bomb for the very first time.

"Jesus, Mom!"

"What?" My mother has this bright, smiling, hard tone that she always uses when she wants me to face facts. She was using it now. "All I'm saying is here you are, miserable, running away from New York, getting into a bad place with Eric, and for what? You're getting older, you're not taking advantage of the city, why do this to yourself?"

This was exactly the one thing I had come to Austin to *not* talk about. I should have known my mother would dig in like a goddamned rat terrier.

I had gone to New York like everybody else goes to New York—just as the essential first step for a potato destined for soup is to have its skin peeled off, the essential starting point for an aspiring actor is to move to New York. I preferred jobs that did not require auditions, which, since I neither looked like Renée Zellweger nor was a terribly good actor, proved to be a problem. Mostly what I'd done was temp, for (to name a few): the photocopier contractor for the UN; the Asian American businesses underwriting department at AIG; the vice president of a broadband technology outfit with an amazing office looking out onto the Brooklyn Bridge, which folded about two weeks after I got there; and an investment firm specializing in the money matters of nunneries. Recently, I'd started work at a government agency downtown. It looked like they were going to offer to bring me on permanently—eventually all the temp employers offered to let you go perm—and for the first time, I was considering, in a despairing sort of way, doing it. It was enough to make me suicidal even before my mom started telling me I was getting old. Mom should have known this, but instead of apologizing for her cruelty she just popped another piece of fried okra into her mouth and said, "Let's go shopping—your clothes are just awful!"

The next morning I lingered at my parents' kitchen table long after they'd both left for work, wrapped up in a well-worn gray flannel robe I'd forgotten I had, sipping coffee. I'd finished the *Times* crossword and all the sections except for Business and Circuits, but didn't yet have enough caffeine in my system to contemplate getting dressed. (I'd overindulged in margaritas the night before, not at all an unusual occurrence when visiting the folks in Austin.) The pantry door stood ajar, and my aimless gaze rested on the bookshelves inside, the familiar ranks of spines lined up there. When I got up to fill my cup one last time, I made a detour and took one of the books—*Mastering the Art of French Cooking, Vol. 1*, my mom's old 1967 edition, a book that had known my family's kitchen longer than I had. I sat back down at the table at which I'd eaten a thousand childhood afternoon snacks and began flipping through, just for the hell of it.

When I was a kid, I used to look at *MtAoFC* quite a lot. Partly it was just my obsession with anything between two covers, but there was something else, too. Because this book has the power to shock. *MtAoFC* is still capable of striking deep if obscure zones of discomfort. Find the most pale, pierced and kohl-eyed, proudly pervy hipster you can and ask her to cook Pâté de Canard en Croûte, aided only by the helpful illustrations on pages 571 through 575. I promise you, she'll be fleeing back to Williamsburg, where no one's going to make her bone a whole duck, faster than you can say, "trucker hats are *soooo* five minutes ago."

But why? What is it about this book? It's just an old cookbook, for God's sake. Yet vegetarians, Atkinsers, and South Beach bums flare their nostrils at the stink of apostasy between its covers. Self-proclaimed foodies spare a smile of fond condescension before returning to their Chez Panisse cookbooks. By all rights, I should feel this way too. I am, after all, that ultimate synthesis of urban flakiness and suburban self-righteousness, the New York actress.

Well, actually, I guess I can't say that, since I've never had a real acting job. And to tell the truth—it's time I faced facts here—I never really even tried. But if I'm not a New York actress, what am I? I'm a person who takes a subway from the outer boroughs to a lower Manhattan office every morning, who spends her days answering phones and doing copying, who is too disconsolate when she gets back to her apartment at night to do anything but sit on the couch and stare vacantly at reality TV shows until she falls asleep.

Oh God. It really was true, wasn't it? I really was a secretary.

When I looked up from *MtAoFC* for the first time, half an hour after I opened it, I realized that deep down, I'd been resigned to being a secretary for months—maybe even years.

That was the bad news. The good news was that the buzzing in my head and queasy but somehow exhilarating squeeze deep in my belly were reminding me that I might still, after all, be something else.

Do you know *Mastering the Art of French Cooking*? You must, at least, know *of* it—it's a cultural landmark, for Pete's sake. Even if you just think of it as the book by that lady who looks like Dan Aykroyd and bleeds a lot, you know *of* it. But do you know the book itself? Try to get your hands on one of the early hardback editions—they're not exactly rare. For a while there, every American housewife who could boil water had a copy, or so I've heard.

It's not lushly illustrated; there are no shiny soft-core images of the glossy-haired author sinking her teeth into a juicy strawberry or smiling stonily before a perfectly rustic tart with carving knife in hand, like some chilly blonde kitchen dominatrix. The dishes are hopelessly dated—the cooking times outrageously long, the use of butter and cream beyond the pale, and not a single reference to pancetta or sea salt or wasabi. This book hasn't been on the must-have list for enterprising gourmands in decades. But as I held it in my hands that morning, opened its cover spangled with tomato-colored fleurs-de-lis, skimmed through its yellowed pages, I felt like I'd at last found something *important*. Why? I bent again over the book's pages, searching for the cause of this strange feeling. It wasn't the food exactly. If you looked hard enough, the food started to feel almost beside the point. No, there was something deeper here, some code within the words, perhaps some secret embedded in the paper itself.

I have never looked to religion for comfort—belief is just not in my genes. But reading *Mastering the Art of French Cooking*—childishly simple and dauntingly complex, incantatory and comforting—I thought this was what prayer must feel like. Sustenance bound up with anticipation and want. Reading *MtAoFC* was like reading pornographic Bible verses.

So naturally when I flew back to New York that May, I had Mom's copy of the book stashed in my bag.

The thing you learn with Potage Parmentier is that "simple" is not exactly the same as "easy." It had never occurred to me that there was a difference until Eric and I sat down on our couch the night of my appointment at the gynecologist's, three months after stealing my mother's forty-year-old cookbook, and took our first slurps of Julia Child's potato soup.

Certainly I had made *easier* dinners. Unwrapping a cellophane-swathed hunk of London broil and tossing it under the broiler was one method that came immediately to mind. Ordering pizza and getting drunk on Stoli gimlets while waiting for it to arrive, that was another favorite. Potage Parmentier didn't even hold a candle, in the easy department.

First you peel a couple of potatoes and slice them up. Slice some leeks, rinse them a couple of times to get rid of the grit—leeks are muddy little suckers. Throw these two ingredients in a pot with some water and some salt. Simmer it for forty-five minutes or so, then either "mash the vegetables in the soup with a fork" or pass them through a food mill. I didn't have a food mill, and I wasn't about to mash up vegetables with a *fork*. What I had was a potato ricer.

Well, technically it was Eric's potato ricer. Before we were married, years ago, before Atkins hit, mashed potatoes used to be Eric's specialty. For a while, before we learned the value of Brooklyn storage space, we'd had this tradition where I'd get him arcane kitchen gadgets, the not-very-funny joke being that he didn't actually cook at all, except for the mashed potatoes. The ricer is the only survivor from this period. It was his Christmas present the year we were in the railroad apartment on Eleventh between Seventh and Eighth—this was before we got priced out of Park Slope entirely. I'd sewn stockings for the both of us out of felt—his is red with white trim, mine white with red—from a pattern in the *Martha Stewart Living* holiday issue that year. We still have them, even though I can't sew and they're totally kattywhompus: the stitching uneven, the decorative cuffs bunched and crooked. They're also way too small for things like ricers. I stuffed it in anyway. Hanging on the mantel of the nonfunctional fireplace in the bedroom, the stocking looked like Santa had brought Eric a Luger. I've never been much good at stocking stuffers.

Once the leeks and potatoes have simmered for an hour or so, you mash them up with a fork or a food mill or a potato ricer. All three of these options are far more of a pain in the neck than the Cuisinart—one of which space-munching behemoths we scored when we got married—but Julia Child allows as how a Cuisinart will turn soup into "something un-French and monotonous." Any suggestion that uses the construction "un-French" is up for debate, but if you make Potage Parmentier, you will see her point. If you use the ricer, the soup will have *bits*—green bits and white bits and yellow bits—instead of being utterly smooth. After you've mushed it up, just stir in a couple of hefty chunks of butter, and you're done. JC says sprinkle with parsley but you don't have to. It looks pretty enough as it is, and it smells glorious, which is funny when you think about it. There's not a thing in it but leeks, potatoes, butter, water, pepper, and salt.

One interesting thing to meditate on while you're making this soup is potatoes. There's something about peeling a potato. Not to say that it's *fun*, exactly. But there's something about scraping off the skin, and rinsing off the dirt, and chopping it into cubes before immersing the cubes in cold water because they'll turn pink if you let them sit out in the air. Something about knowing exactly what you're doing, and why. Potatoes have been potatoes for a long, long time, and people have treated them in just this way, toward the end of making just such a soup. There is clarity in the act of peeling a potato, a winnowing down to one sure, true way. And even if afterward you do push it through some gadget you got at Crate and Barrel, the peeling is still a part of what you do, the first thing.

I was supposed to have spent my twenties (a) hammering away for ninety hours a week at some high-paying, ethically dubious job, drinking heavily, and having explosive sex with a rich array of twenty-something men; (b) awaking at noon every day in my Williamsburg loft to work on my painting/poetry/knitting/performance art, easily shaking off the effects of stylish drugs and tragically hip clubs and explosive sex with a rich array of twenty-something men (and women if I could manage it); or (c) pursuing higher education, sweating bullets over an obscure dissertation and punctuating my intellectual throes with some pot and explosive sex with a rich array of professors and undergrads. These were the models, for someone like me.

But I did none of these things. Instead, I got married. I didn't mean to, exactly. It just kind of happened.

Eric and I were high school sweethearts. Wait, it gets worse. We were in a high school *play* together. Our courtship was straight out of one of the ickier films from the John Hughes oeuvre, *Some Kind of Wonderful*, maybe—all kinds of misunderstandings and jealous boyfriends and angst-ridden stage kisses. In other words, the sort of too-typical high school romance that people of our generation are meant to get over and cover up later on. But we didn't. Somehow we never got around to the breaking-up part. At the age of twenty-four, when we were still sleeping together and reasonably satisfied with the whole toilet-seat-and-toothpaste-cap situation, we went ahead and got married.

Please understand—I love my husband like a pig loves shit. Maybe even more. But in the circles I run in, being married for more than five years before reaching the age of thirty ranks real high on the list of most socially damaging traits, right below watching NASCAR and listening to Shania Twain. I'm used to getting questions like "Is he the only person you've ever had sex with?" or, even more insultingly, "Are *you* the only person *he's* ever had sex with?"

All this to say that sometimes I get a little defensive. Even with Isabel, who I've known since kindergarten, and Sally, my freshman-year roommate, and Gwen, who comes over to eat at our apartment every weekend and *adores* Eric. I would confess to none of them the thing I sometimes think, which is: "Eric can be a little pushy." I couldn't hack the hastily smothered expressions of dismay and smug I-told-you-so eyebrows; I know my friends would imagine something between *The Stepford Wives* and a domestic abuse PSA narrated by J-Lo. But I mean neither shoving matches nor domineering at dinner parties. I just mean that he *pushes*. He can't be satisfied with telling me I'm the most gorgeous and talented woman on the planet and that he would die without me, while mixing me a dry Stoli gimlet. No, he has to *encourage*. He has to *make suggestions*. It can be most annoying.

So I made this soup, this Potage Parmentier, from a recipe in a forty-year-old cookbook I'd stolen from my mother the previous spring. And it was good—inexplicably good. We ate it sitting on the couch, bowls perched on knees, the silence broken only by the occasional snort of laughter as we watched a pert blonde high school student dust vampires on the television. In almost no time we were slurping the dregs of our third servings. (It turns out that one reason we're so good together is that each of us eats more and faster than anyone either of us has ever met; also, we both recognize the genius of *Buffy the Vampire Slayer*.) Earlier that evening, after the gynecologist appointment, when I was standing in the Korean deli staring at produce, I'd been thinking, "I'm twenty-nine, I'm never going to have kids or a real job, my husband will leave me and I'll die alone in an outer-borough hovel with twenty cats and it'll take two weeks for the stench to reach the hall." But now, three bowls of potato soup later, I was, to my relief, thinking of nothing much at all. I lay on my back on the couch, quietly digesting. Julia Child's soup had made me vulnerable.

Eric saw an in, and took it.

"That was good, honey."

I sighed my agreement.

"Real good. And there wasn't even any meat in it."

(Eric is a sensitive twenty-first-century sort of guy, but a Texan nevertheless, and the idea of a dinner without animal flesh gets him a little panicky.)

"You're such a good cook, Julie. Maybe you should go to culinary school."

I'd started cooking in college, basically to keep Eric in my thrall. In the years since, though, the whole thing had blown a little out of proportion. I don't know if Eric felt pride that he had introduced me to my consuming passion, or guilt that my urge to satisfy his innocent liking for escargot and rhubarb had metastasized into an unhealthy obsession. Whatever the reason, this thing about cooking school had developed into one of our habitual dead-end alleys of conversation. I was too deliciously idle after my soup to get ticked off about it, and just snorted quietly. Even that indication that he had my ear, though, was a tactical error. I knew it as soon as I'd made a sound. I squeezed my eyes shut, feigning sudden sleep or deafness.

"Seriously. You could go to the Culinary Institute! We could move out to the Hudson Valley, and you could just spend all your time learning to be a chef."

And then, no sooner than I'd cautioned myself against it, I made tactical error #2: "They won't let me in without professional experience. I'd have to go peel potatoes for two-fifty an hour for six months. You want to support me with all your big bucks while I do that?"

Giving in to the enticing prospect of emasculating my husband. Always, always a mistake.

"Maybe some other school to start, then—somewhere here in the city?"

"We can't afford it."

Eric didn't answer. He sat quietly on the edge of the couch with his hand on my shin. I thought about kicking it off, but the shin seemed a neutral enough spot. One of the cats jumped up onto my chest, sniffed my breath, then stalked off stiff-legged, her mouth open in faint disgust.

"If I wanted to learn to cook, I'd just cook my way through *Mastering the Art of French Cooking*."

It was an odd sort of statement to make drip with sarcasm, but I managed it anyway. Eric just sat there.

"Not that it would do me any good, of course. Can't get a job out of that."

"At least we'd eat good for a while."

Now I was the one who said nothing for a moment, because of course he was right about that.

"I'd be exhausted all the time. I'd get fat. We'd have to eat brains. And eggs. I don't eat eggs, Eric. You know I don't eat eggs."

"No. You don't."

"It's a stupid idea."

Eric said nothing for a while. *Buffy* had ended and the news was on—a correspondent was standing on a flooded street in Sheepshead Bay, saying something about a broken water main. We sat on the couch in our stuffy Bay Ridge living room, staring at the screen as if we gave a damn. All around us teetered towers of boxes, the looming reminder of our upcoming move.

When I look back on it now, it is as if I could actually hear the taut creak of a fisherman giving out just a tiny bit of line when Eric said: "You could start a blog."

I cut my eyes over to him in irritation, a massive white-skinned shark thrashing its tail.

"Julie. You *do* know what a *blog* is, don't you?"

Of course I didn't know what a blog was. It was August of 2002. Nobody knew about blogs, except for a few guys like Eric who spend their days using company computers to pursue the zeitgeist. No issue of domestic or international policy was too big, no pop-culture backwater too obscure; from the War on Terror to *Fear Factor*, it was all one big, beautiful sliding scale for Eric.

"You know, like a Web site sort of thing. Only it's easy. You don't have to know anything about anything."

"Sounds perfect for me."

"About computers, I mean."

"Are you going to make me that drink, or what?"

"Sure."

And he did. He left me alone. He was free to, now that he knew the hook was sunk.

Lulled by the calming music of ice clattering in the cocktail shaker, I began to ponder; this life we had going for ourselves, Eric and I, it felt like the opposite of Potage Parmentier. It was easy enough to keep on with the soul-sucking jobs; at least it saved having to make a choice. But how much longer could I take such an easy life? Quicksand was easy. Hell, death was easy. Maybe that's why my synapses had started snapping at the sight of potatoes and leeks in the Korean deli. Maybe that was what was plucking deep down in my belly whenever I thought of Julia Child's book. Maybe I needed to make like a potato, winnow myself down, be a part of something that was not easy, just simple.

Just then Eric emerged again from the kitchen, carrying two Stoli gimlets. He handed off one of the glasses to me, carefully, so as not to spill anything over those treacherous martini lips, and I took a sip. Eric always made the best gimlets—icy cold, very dry, with an almost-not-there shade of chartreuse lingering in their slightly oily depths.

"Okay," I said, taking another sip as Eric sat down beside me. "Tell me again about this blog thing?"

And so, late that evening, a tiny line dropped into the endless sea of cyberspace, the slenderest of lures in the blackest of waters.

THE BOOK
Mastering the Art of French Cooking. First edition, 1961. Louisette Bertholle. Simone Beck. And, of course, Julia Child, the woman who taught America to cook, and to eat. Today we think we live in the world Alice Waters made, but beneath it all is Julia, and no one can touch her.

THE CONTENDER
Government drone by day, renegade foodie by night. Too old for theater, too young for children, and too bitter for anything else, Julie Powell was looking for a challenge. And in the Julie/Julia Project she found it. Risking her marriage, her job, and her cats' well-being, she has signed on for a deranged assignment. 365 days. 524 recipes. One girl and a crappy outer-borough kitchen. How far it will go, no one can say . . .

It wasn't much—nearly nothing, in fact. Not even so much as a recipe for potato soup. A few words strung together, is all. But together, out there, they seemed perhaps to glow, only faintly. Just enough.

Julie and Julia, Powell's blog-turned-book-turned-movie helped revitalize sales of Julia Child's *Mastering the Art of French Cooking*. Powell claims that "the dishes" in this cookbook "are hopelessly dated." Locate a copy of *Mastering the Art of French Cooking* and study Child's Potage Parmentier. Compare her recipe with a more modern version of potato and leek soup (you might look, for instance, in Alice Waters's *The Art of Simple Food* or at a recipe site online). Does Child's recipe feel dated next to the newer version? If so, how do the two differ? How much information does each author provide? How is the information composed on the page? Describe the style of each writer. Are there distinctive word choices in either? Do the authors' tones differ? Who are the audiences for each of the recipes? How might that effect the presentation of the material?

Both Powell and David Sedaris in "Tasteless" end their food memoirs with the concept of "enough." To what ends does each author use "enough"? How does each define it? Why do you think "enough" concludes both of these two personal food narratives?

Powell develops a Potage Parmentier metaphor throughout her chapter and concludes, "Maybe I needed to make like a potato, winnow myself down, be a part of something that was not easy, just simple." With a group of classmates, discuss what kinds of extended food metaphors might be fitting for your lives.

A graduate of the highly respected Culinary Institute of America, Anthony Bourdain is a chef, author, and now television star—thanks in large part to the Travel Channel program "No Reservations" and his appearances as a guest judge on Bravo's "Top Chef." In 1999, The New Yorker published "Don't Eat Before Reading This," an exposé of New York City restaurants that led to the 2000 book Kitchen Confidential: Adventures in the Culinary Underbelly. *"Food is Good" and "Who Cooks?" (which starts on page 93) are excerpts from* Kitchen Confidential.

FOOD IS GOOD

BY ANTHONY BOURDAIN

My first indication that food was something other than a substance one stuffed in one's face when hungry—like filling up at a gas station—came after fourth-grade elementary school. It was on a family vacation to Europe, on the *Queen Mary*, in the cabin-class dining room. There's a picture somewhere: my mother in her Jackie O sunglasses, my younger brother and I in our painfully cute cruisewear, boarding the big Cunard ocean liner, all of us excited about our first transatlantic voyage, our first trip to my father's ancestral homeland, France.

It was the soup.
It was *cold*.

This was something of a discovery for a curious fourth-grader whose entire experience of soup to this point had consisted of Campbell's cream of tomato and chicken noodle. I'd eaten in restaurants before, sure, but this was the first food I really noticed. It was the first food I enjoyed and, more important, remembered enjoying. I asked our patient British waiter what this delightfully cool, tasty liquid was.

"Vichyssoise," came the reply, a word that to this day—even though it's now a tired old warhorse of a menu selection and one I've prepared thousands of times—still has a magical ring to it. I remember everything about the experience: the way our waiter ladled it from a silver tureen into my bowl, the crunch of tiny chopped chives he spooned on as garnish, the rich, creamy taste of leek and potato, the pleasurable shock, the surprise that it was cold.

I don't remember much else about the passage across the Atlantic. I saw *Boeing Boeing* with Jerry Lewis and Tony Curtis in the *Queen*'s movie theater, and a Bardot flick. The old liner shuddered and groaned and vibrated terribly the whole way—barnacles on the hull was the official explanation—and from New York to Cherbourg, it was like riding atop a giant lawnmower. My brother and I quickly became bored, and spent much of our time in the "Teen Lounge," listening to "House of the Rising Sun" on the jukebox, or watching the water slosh around like a contained tidal wave in the below-deck salt-water pool.

But that cold soup stayed with me. It resonated, waking me up, making me aware of my tongue, and in some way, preparing me for future events.

My second pre-epiphany in my long climb to chefdom also came during that first trip to France. After docking, my mother, brother and I stayed with cousins in the small seaside town of Cherbourg, a bleak, chilly resort area in Normandy, on the English Channel. The sky was almost always cloudy; the water was inhospitably cold. All the neighborhood kids thought I knew Steve McQueen and John Wayne personally—as an American, it was assumed we were all pals, that we hung out together on the range, riding horses and gunning down miscreants—so I enjoyed a certain celebrity right away. The beaches, while no good for swimming, were studded with old Nazi blockhouses and gun emplacements, many still bearing visible bullet scars and the scorch of flamethrowers, and there were tunnels under the dunes—all very cool for a little kid to explore. My little French friends were, I was astonished to find, allowed to have a cigarette on Sunday, were given watered *vin ordinaire* at the dinner table, and best of all, they owned Velo Solex motorbikes. *This* was the way to raise kids, I recall thinking, unhappy that my mother did not agree.

So for my first few weeks in France, I explored underground passageways, looking for dead Nazis, played miniature golf, sneaked cigarettes, read a lot of Tintin and Asterix comics, scooted around on my friends' motorbikes and absorbed little life-lessons from observations that, for instance, the family friend Monsieur Dupont brought his mistress to some meals and his wife to others, his extended brood of children apparently indifferent to the switch.

I was largely unimpressed by the food.

The butter tasted strangely "cheesy" to my undeveloped palate. The milk—a staple, no, a mandatory ritual in '60s American kiddie life—was undrinkable here. Lunch seemed always to consist of sandwich au jambon or croque-monsieur. Centuries of French cuisine had yet to make an impression. What I noticed about food, French style, was what they *didn't* have.

After a few weeks of this, we took a night train to Paris, where we met up with my father, and a spanking new Rover Sedan Mark III, our touring car. In Paris, we stayed at the Hôtel Lutétia, then a large, slightly shabby old pile on Boulevard Haussmann. The menu selections for my brother and me expanded somewhat, to include steak-frites and steak haché (hamburger). We did all the predictable touristy things: climbed the Tour Eiffel, picnicked in the Bois de Boulogne, marched past the Great Works at the Louvre, pushed toy sailboats around the fountain in the Jardin de Luxembourg—none of it much fun for a nine-year-old with an already developing criminal bent. My principal interest at this time was adding to my collection of English translations of Tintin adventures. Hergé's crisply drafted tales of drug-smuggling, ancient temples, and strange and far-away places and culture were *real* exotica for me. I prevailed on my poor parents to buy hundreds of dollars-worth of these stories at W. H. Smith, the English bookstore, just to keep me from whining about the deprivations of France. With my little short-shorts a permanent affront, I was quickly becoming a sullen, moody, difficult little bastard. I fought constantly with my brother, carped about everything, and was in every possible way a drag on my mother's Glorious Expedition.

My parents did their best. They took us everywhere, from restaurant to restaurant, cringing, no doubt, every time we insisted on steak haché (with ketchup, no less) and a "Coca." They endured silently my gripes about cheesy butter, the seemingly endless amusement I took in advertisements for a popular soft drink of the time, Pschitt. "I want shit! I want shit!" They managed to ignore the eye-rolling and fidgeting when they spoke French, tried to encourage me to find something, anything, to enjoy.

And there came a time when, finally, they *didn't* take the kids along.

I remember it well, because it was such a slap in the face. It was a wake-up call that food could be important, a challenge to my natural belligerence. By being denied, a door opened.

The town's name was Vienne. We'd driven miles and miles of road to get there. My brother and I were fresh out of Tintins and cranky as hell. The French countryside, with its graceful, tree-lined roads, hedgerows, tilled fields and picture-book villages provided little distraction. My folks had by now endured weeks of relentless complaining through many tense and increasingly unpleasant meals. They'd dutifully ordered our steak haché, crudités variées, sandwich au jambon and the like long enough. They'd put up with our grousing that the beds were too hard, the pillows too soft, the neck-rolls and toilets and plumbing too weird. They'd even allowed us a little watered wine, as it was clearly the French thing to do—but also, I think, to shut us up. They'd taken my brother and me, the two Ugliest Little Americans, everywhere.

Vienne was different.

They pulled the gleaming new Rover into the parking lot of a restaurant called, rather promisingly, La Pyramide, handed us what was apparently a hoarded stash of Tintins . . . *and then left us in the car!*

It was a hard blow. Little brother and I were left in that car for over three hours, an eternity for two miserable kids already bored out of their minds. I had plenty of time to wonder: *What could be so great inside those walls?* They were eating in there. I knew that. And it was certainly a Big Deal; even at a witless age nine, I could recognize the nervous anticipation, the excitement, the near-reverence with which my beleaguered parents had approached this hour. And I had the Vichyssoise Incident still fresh in my mind. Food, it appeared, could be *important.* It could be an event. It had secrets.

I know now, of course, that La Pyramide, even in 1966, was the center of the culinary universe. Bocuse, Troisgros, *everybody* had done their time there, making their bones under the legendarily fearsome proprietor, Ferdinand Point. Point was the Grand Master of cuisine at the time, and La Pyramide was Mecca for foodies. This was a pilgrimage for my earnestly Francophile parents. In some small way, I got that through my tiny, empty skull in the back of the sweltering parked car, even then.

Things changed. *I* changed after that.

First of all, I was furious. Spite, always a great motivating force in my life, caused me to become suddenly adventurous where food was concerned. I decided then and there to outdo my foodie parents. At the same time, I could gross out my still uninitiated little brother. I'd show *them* who the gourmet was!

Brains? Stinky, runny cheeses that smelled like dead man's feet? Horsemeat? Sweetbreads? Bring it on!! Whatever had the most shock value became my meal of choice. For the rest of that summer, and in the summers that followed, I ate *everything*. I scooped gooey Vacherin, learned to love the cheesy, rich Normandy butter, especially slathered on baguettes and dipped in bitter hot chocolate. I sneaked red wine whenever possible, tried fritures—tiny whole fish, fried and eaten with persillade—loving that I was eating heads, eyes, bones and all. I ate ray in beurre noisette, saucisson à l'ail, tripes, rogons de veau (kidneys), boudin noir that squirted blood down my chin.

And I had my first oyster.

Now, *this* was a truly significant event. I remember it like I remember losing my virginity—and in many ways, more fondly.

August of that summer was spent in La Teste sur Mer, a tiny oyster village on the Bassin d'Arcachon in the Gironde (Southwest France). We stayed with my aunt, Tante Jeanne, and my uncle, Oncle Gustav, in the same red tile-roofed, white stuccoed house where my father had summered as a boy. My Tante Jeanne was a frumpy, bespectacled, slightly smelly old woman, my Oncle Gustav, a geezer in coveralls and beret who smoked hand-rolled cigarettes until they disappeared onto the tip of his tongue. Little had changed about La Teste in the years since my father had vacationed there. The neighbors were still all oyster fishermen. Their families still raised rabbits and grew tomatoes in their backyards. Houses had two kitchens, an inside one and an outdoor "fish kitchen." There was a hand pump for drinking water from a well, and an outhouse by the rear of the garden. Lizards and snails were everywhere. The main tourist attractions were the nearby Dune of Pyla (Europe's Largest Sand Dune!) and the nearby resort town of Arcachon, where the French flocked in unison for *Les Grandes Vacances*. Television was a Big Event. At seven o'clock, when the two national stations would come on the air, my Oncle Gustav would solemnly emerge from his room with a key chained to his hip and ceremoniously unlock the cabinet doors that covered the screen.

My brother and I were happier here. There was more to do. The beaches were warm, and closer in climate to what we knew back home, with the added attraction of the ubiquitous Nazi blockhouses. There were lizards to hunt down and exterminate with readily available *pétards*, firecrackers which one could buy legally (!) over-the-counter. There was a forest within walking distance where an actual hermit lived, and my brother and I spent hours there, spying on him from the underbrush. By now I could read and enjoy comic books in French and of course I was eating—*really* eating. Murky brown soupe de poisson, tomato salad, moules marinières, poulet basquaise (we were only a few miles from the Basque country). We made day trips to Cap Ferret, a wild, deserted and breathtakingly magnificent Atlantic beach with big rolling waves, taking along baguettes and saucissons and wheels of cheese, wine and Evian (bottled water was at that time unheard of back home). A few miles west was Lac Cazeaux, a fresh-water lake where my brother and I could rent *pédalo* watercraft and pedal our way around the deep. We ate gaufres, delicious hot waffles, covered in whipped cream and powdered sugar. The two hot songs of that summer on the Cazeaux jukebox were "Whiter Shade of Pale" by Procol Harum, and "These Boots Were Made for Walkin'" by Nancy Sinatra. The French played those two songs over and over again, the music punctuated by the sonic booms from French air force jets which would swoop over the lake on their way to a nearby bombing range. With all the rock and roll, good stuff to eat and high-explosives at hand, I was reasonably happy.

So, when our neighbor, Monsieur Saint-Jour, the oyster fisherman, invited my family out on his *penas* (oyster boat), I was enthusiastic.

At six in the morning, we boarded Monsieur Saint-Jour's small wooden vessel with our picnic baskets and our sensible footwear. He was a crusty old bastard, dressed like my uncle in ancient denim coveralls, espadrilles and beret. He had a leathery, tanned and windblown face, hollow cheeks, and the tiny broken blood vessels on nose and cheeks that everyone seemed to have from drinking so much of the local Bordeaux. He hadn't fully briefed his guests on what was involved in these daily travails. We put-putted out to a buoy marking his underwater oyster *parc*, a fenced-off section of bay bottom, and we sat . . . and sat . . . and sat, in the roaring August sun, waiting for the tide to go out. The idea was to float the boat over the stockade fence walls, then sit there until the boat slowly sank with the water level, until it rested on the *bassin* floor. At this point, Monsieur Saint-Jour, and his guests presumably, would rake the oysters, collect a few good specimens for sale in port, and remove any parasites that might be endangering his crop.

There was, I recall, still about two feet of water left to go before the hull of the boat settled on dry ground and we could walk about the *parc*. We'd already polished off the Brie and baguettes and downed the Evian, but I was still hungry, and characteristically said so.

Monsieur Saint-Jour, on hearing this—as if challenging his American passengers—inquired in his thick Girondais accent, if any of us would care to try an oyster.

My parents hesitated. I doubt they'd realized they might have to actually *eat* one of the raw, slimy things we were currently floating over. My little brother recoiled in horror.

But I, in the proudest moment of my young life, stood up smartly, grinning with defiance, and volunteered to be the first.

And in that unforgettably sweet moment in my personal history, that one moment still more alive for me than so many of the other "firsts" which followed—first pussy, first joint, first day in high school, first published book, or any other thing—I attained glory. Monsieur Saint-Jour beckoned me over to the gunwale, where he leaned over, reached down until his head nearly disappeared underwater, and emerged holding a single silt-encrusted oyster, huge and irregularly shaped, in his rough, clawlike fist. With a snubby, rust-covered oyster knife, he popped the thing open and handed it to me, everyone watching now, my little brother shrinking away from this glistening, vaguely sexual-looking object, still dripping and nearly alive.

I took it in my hand, tilted the shell back into my mouth as instructed by the by now beaming Monsieur Saint-Jour, and with one bite and a slurp, wolfed it down. It tasted of seawater . . . of brine and flesh . . . and somehow . . . of the future.

Everything was different now. Everything.

I'd not only survived—I'd *enjoyed*.

This, I knew, was the magic I had until now been only dimly and spitefully aware of. I was hooked. My parents' shudders, my little brother's expression of unrestrained revulsion and amazement only reinforced the sense that I had, somehow, become a man. I had had an *adventure*, tasted forbidden fruit, and everything that followed in my life—the food, the long and often stupid and self-destructive chase for *the next thing*, whether it was drugs or sex or some other new sensation—would all stem from this moment.

I'd learned something. Viscerally, instinctively, spiritually—even in some small, precursive way, sexually—and there was no turning back. The genie was out of the bottle. My life as a cook, and as a chef, had begun.

Food had *power*.

It could inspire, astonish, shock, excite, delight and *impress*. It had the power to please me . . . and others. This was valuable information.

For the rest of that summer, and in later summers, I'd often slip off by myself to the little stands by the port, where one could buy brown paper bags of unwashed, black-covered oysters by the dozen. After a few lessons from my new soul-mate, blood brother and bestest buddy, Monsieur Saint-Jour—who was now sharing his after-work bowls of sugared *vin ordinaire* with me too—I could easily open the oysters by myself, coming in from behind with the knife and popping the hinge like it was Aladdin's cave.

I'd sit in the garden among the tomatoes and the lizards and eat my oysters and drink Kronenbourgs (France was a wonderland for under-age drinkers), happily reading *Modesty Blaise* and the *Katzenjammer Kids* and the lovely hard-bound *bandes dessinées* in French, until the pictures swam in front of my eyes, smoking the occasional pilfered Gitane. And I still associate the taste of oysters with those heady, wonderful days of illicit late-afternoon buzzes. The smell of French cigarettes, the taste of beer, that unforgettable feeling of doing something I shouldn't be doing.

I had, as yet, no plans to cook professionally. But I frequently look back at my life, searching for that fork in the road, trying to figure out where, exactly, I *went bad* and became a thrill-seeking, pleasure-hungry sensualist, always looking to shock, amuse, terrify and manipulate, seeking to fill that empty spot in my soul with something new.

I like to think it was Monsieur Saint-Jour's fault. But of course, it was me all along.

In this excerpt and on his Travel Channel television show "No Reservations," Bourdain constructs a particular persona. Find and watch an episode of "No Reservations." How might you characterize his tone in these pieces? How does the voice he constructs differ from previous food writers you've read and food shows you've watched? What stylistic tools does he brandish to achieve this effect in his writing and in his performance?

Bourdain's awakening to a life of food culminates in his epiphany that "food had power." What does he mean by this? How does Bourdain define power here? Have you experienced anything in your life that compares to the way Bourdain talks about food?

As in Bourdain's narrative, childhood experiences with food can leave a lasting imprint. Even after decades of cooking experience, vichyssoise, Bourdain's first encounter with extraordinary food, has a "magical ring" to it. Compose a brief essay in which you describe a formative or memorable childhood food experience. (Your instructor may have you use this exercise as a starting point for a longer food memoir.)

FOOD

Journalist and author Bill Buford's fascination with chef Mario Batali led to the 2006 book Heat: An Amateur's Adventures as Kitchen Slave, Line Cook, Pasta-Maker, and Apprentice to a Dante-Quoting Butcher in Tuscany. *"Dinner with Mario" opens the book, which, among other things, "accurately and hilariously describes the painfully acquired techniques of the professional cook," according to a review by Anthony Bourdain.*

DINNER WITH MARIO

BY BILL BUFORD

A human being is primarily a bag for putting food into; the other functions and faculties may be more godlike, but in point of time they come afterwards. A man dies and is buried, and all his words and actions are forgotten, but the food he has eaten lives after him in the sound or rotten bones of his children. I think it could be plausibly argued that changes of diet are more important than changes of dynasty or even of religion. The Great War, for instance, could never have happened if tinned food had not been invented. And the history of the past four hundred years in England would have been immensely different if it had not been for the introduction of root-crops and various other vegetables at the end of the Middle Ages, and a little later the introduction of non-alcoholic drinks (tea, coffee, cocoa) and also of distilled liquors to which the beer-drinking English were not accustomed. Yet it is curious how seldom the all-importance of food is recognized. You see statues everywhere to politicians, poets, bishops, but none to cooks or bacon-curers or market gardeners.

--George Orwell, *The Road to Wigan Pier*

The first glimpse I had of what Mario Batali's friends had described to me as the "myth of Mario" was on a cold Saturday night in January 2002, when I invited him to a birthday dinner. Batali, the chef and co-owner of Babbo, an Italian restaurant in Manhattan, is such a famous and proficient cook that he's rarely invited to people's homes for a meal, he told me, and he went out of his way to be a grateful guest. He arrived bearing his own quince-flavored grappa (the rough, distilled end-of-harvest grape juice rendered almost drinkable by the addition of the fruit); a jar of homemade *nocino* (same principle, but

Chef Mario Batali

with walnuts); an armful of wine; and a white, dense slab of *lardo*—literally, the raw "lardy" back of a very fat pig, one he'd cured himself with herbs and salt. I was what might generously be described as an enthusiastic cook, more confident than competent (that is, keen but fundamentally clueless), and to this day I am astonished that I had the nerve to ask over someone of Batali's reputation, along with six guests who thought they'd have an amusing evening witnessing my humiliation. (Mario was a friend of the birthday friend, so I'd thought—why not invite him, too?—but when, wonder of wonders, he then accepted and I told my wife, Jessica, she was apoplectic with wonder: "What in the world were you thinking of, inviting a famous chef to our apartment for *dinner*?")

In the event, there was little comedy, mainly because Mario didn't give me a chance. Shortly after my being instructed that only a moron would let his meat rest by wrapping it in foil after cooking it, I cheerfully gave up and let Batali tell me what to do. By then he'd taken over the evening, anyway. Not long into it, he'd cut the *lardo* into thin slices and, with a startling flourish of intimacy, laid them individually on our tongues, whispering that we needed to let the fat melt in our mouths to appreciate its intensity. The *lardo* was from a pig that, in the last months of its seven-hundred-and-fifty-pound life, had lived on apples, walnuts, and cream ("The best song sung in the key of pig"), and Mario convinced us that, as the fat dissolved, we'd detect the flavors of the animal's happy diet—there, in the back of the mouth. No one that evening had knowingly eaten pure fat before ("At the restaurant, I tell the waiters to call it prosciutto bianco"), and by the time Mario had persuaded us to a third helping everyone's heart was racing. Batali was an impressively dedicated drinker—he mentioned in passing that, on trips to Italy made with his Babbo co-owner, Joe Bastianich, the two of them had been known to put away a case of wine during an evening meal—and while I don't think that any of us drank anything like that, we were, by now, very thirsty (the *lardo*, the salt, the human heat of so much jollity) and, cheered on, found ourselves knocking back more and more. I don't know. I don't really remember. There were also the grappa and the *nocino*, and one of my last images is of Batali at three in the morning—a stoutly round man with his back dangerously arched, his eyes closed, a long red ponytail swinging rhythmically behind him, an unlit cigarette dangling from his mouth, his red Converse high-tops pounding the floor—playing air guitar to Neil Young's "Southern Man." Batali was forty-one, and I remember thinking it had been a long time since I'd seen a grown man play air guitar. He then found the soundtrack for *Buena Vista Social Club*, tried to salsa with one of the women guests (who promptly fell over a sofa), moved on to her boyfriend, who was unresponsive, put on a Tom Waits CD instead, and sang along as he washed the dishes and swept the floor. He reminded me of an arrangement we'd made for the next day—when I'd invited Batali to dinner, he'd reciprocated by asking me to join him at a New York Giants football game, tickets courtesy of the commissioner of the NFL, who had just eaten at Babbo—and then disappeared with three of my friends, assuring them that, with his back-of-the-hand knowledge of downtown establishments open until five, he'd find a place to continue the evening. They ended up at Marylou's in the Village—in Batali's description, "A wise guy joint where you can get anything at any time of night, and none of it good."

It was daylight when Batali got home. I learned this from his building superintendent the next morning, as the two of us tried to get Batali to wake up—the commissioner's driver was waiting outside. When Batali finally appeared, forty-five minutes later, he was momentarily perplexed, standing in the doorway of his apartment in his underwear and wondering why I was there, too. (Batali has a remarkable girth, and it was startling to see him clad so.) Then, in minutes, he transformed himself into what I would come to know as the Batali look: the shorts, the clogs, the wraparound sunglasses, the red hair pulled back into its ponytail. One moment, a rotund Clark Kent in his underpants; the next, "*Molto* Mario"—the clever, many-layered name of his cooking television program, which, in one of its senses, literally means *Very* Mario (that is, an *intensified* Mario, an *exaggerated* Mario)—and a figure whose renown I didn't appreciate until, as guests of the commissioner, we were allowed onto the field before the game. Fans of the New York Giants are so famously brutish as to be cartoons (bare-chested on a wintry morning or wearing hard hats; in any case, not guys putting in their domestic duty in the kitchen), and I was surprised by how many recognized the ponytailed chef, who stood facing them, arms crossed over his chest, beaming. "Hey, Molto!" they shouted. "What's cooking, Mario?" "Mario, make me a pasta!" At the time, *Molto Mario* was shown on afternoons on cable television, and I found a complex picture of the working metropolitan male emerging, one rushing home the moment his shift ended to catch lessons in braising his broccoli rabe and getting just the right forked texture on his homemade orecchiette. I stood back with one of the security people, taking in the spectacle (by now members of the crowd were chanting "Molto, Molto, Molto")—this very round man, whose manner and dress said, "Dude, where's the party?"

"I love this guy," the security man said. "Just lookin' at him makes me hungry."

Mario Batali is the most recognized chef in a city with more chefs than any other city in the world. In addition to Batali's television show—and his appearances promoting, say, the NASCAR race track in Delaware—he was simply and energetically omnipresent. It would be safe to say that no New York chef ate more, drank more, and was out and about as much. If you live in New York City, you will see him eventually (sooner, if your evenings get going around two in the morning). With his partner, Joe, Batali also owned two other restaurants, Esca and Lupa, and a shop selling Italian wine, and, when we met, they were talking about opening a pizzeria and buying a vineyard in Tuscany. But Babbo was the heart of their enterprise, crushed into what was originally a nineteenth-century coach house, just off Washington Square, in Greenwich Village. The building was narrow; the space was crowded, jostly, and loud; and the food, studiously Italian, rather than Italian-American, was characterized by an over-the-top flourish that seemed to be expressly Batali's. People went there in the expectation of excess. Sometimes I wondered if Batali was less a conventional cook than an advocate of a murkier enterprise of stimulating outrageous appetites (whatever they might be) and satisfying them intensely (by whatever means). A friend of mine, who'd once dropped by the bar for a drink and was then fed personally by Batali for the next six hours, went on a diet of soft fruit and water for three days. "This guy knows no middle ground. It's just excess on a level I've never known before—it's food and drink, food and drink, food and drink, until you feel you're on drugs." Chefs who were regular visitors were subjected to extreme versions of what was already an extreme experience. "We're going to kill him," Batali said to me with maniacal glee as he prepared a meal for a rival who had innocently ordered a seven-course tasting menu, to which Batali added a lethal number of extra courses. The starters (all variations in pig) included *lonza* (the cured backstrap from the cream-apple-and-walnut herd), *coppa* (from the shoulder), a fried foot, a porcini mushroom roasted with

Batali's own *pancetta* (the belly), plus ("for the hell of it") a pasta topped with a *guanciale* (the jowls). This year, Mario was trying out a new motto: "Wretched excess is just barely enough."

Batali was born in 1960 and grew up outside Seattle: a suburban kid with a solid *Leave It to Beaver* upbringing. His mother, Marilyn, is English and French Canadian—from her comes her son's flaming red hair and a fair, un-Italian complexion. The Italian is from his father, Armandino, the grandson of immigrants who arrived in the 1890s. When Mario was growing up, his father was a well-paid Boeing executive in charge of procuring airplane parts made overseas, and in 1975, after being posted to Europe, to supervise the manufacturing close-up, he moved his family to Spain. That, according to Gina, Mario's youngest sibling, was when Mario changed. ("He was already pushing the limits.") Madrid, in the post-Franco years (bars with no minimum age, hash hangouts, the world's oldest profession suddenly legalized), was a place of exhilarating license, and Mario seems to have experienced a little bit of everything on offer. He was caught growing marijuana on the roof of his father's apartment building (the first incident of what would become a theme—Batali was later expelled from his dorm in college, suspected of dealing, and, later still, there was some trouble in Tijuana that actually landed him in jail). The marijuana association also evokes a memory of the first meals Batali remembers preparing, late-night *panini* with caramelized locally grown onions, a local cow's-milk Spanish cheese, and paper-thin slices of chorizo: "The best stoner munch you can imagine; me and my younger brother Dana were just classic stoner kids—we were so happy."

By the time Batali returned to the United States in 1978 to attend Rutgers University, in New Jersey, he was determined to get back to Europe ("I wanted to be a Spanish banker—I *loved* the idea of making a lot of money and living a luxurious life in Madrid"), and his unlikely double major was in business management and Spanish theatre. But after being thrown out of his dorm, Batali got work as a dishwasher at a pizzeria called Stuff Yer Face (in its name alone, destiny was calling), and his life changed. He was promoted to cook, then line cook (working at one "station" in a "line" of stations, making one thing), and then asked to be manager, an offer he turned down. He didn't want the responsibility; he was having too good a time. The life at Stuff Yer Face was fast (twenty-five years later, he still claims he has the record for the most pizzas made in an hour), sexy ("The most booooootiful waitresses in town"), and very buzzy ("I don't want to come off as a big druggy, but when a guy comes into the kitchen with a pizza pan turned upside down, covered with lines of coke, how can you say no?"). When, in his junior year, he attended a career conference hosted by representatives from major corporations, Batali realized he had been wrong; he was never going to be a banker. He was going to be a chef.

"My mother and grandmother had always told me that I should be a cook. In fact, when I was preparing my applications for college, my mother had suggested cooking school. But I said, 'Ma, that's too gay. I don't want to go to cooking school—that's for fags.'" Five years later, Batali was back in Europe, attending the Cordon Bleu in London.

His father, still overseeing Boeing's foreign operations, was now based in England. Gina Batali was there, too, and recalls seeing her eldest brother only when she was getting ready for school and he was returning from his all-night escapades after attending classes during the day and then working at a pub. The pub was the Six Bells, on the King's Road in Chelsea. Mario had been bartending at the so-called American bar (*"No idea* what I was doing"), when a high-priced dining room opened in the back and a chef was hired to run it, a Yorkshire man named Marco Pierre White. Batali, bored by the pace of cooking school, was hired to be the new chef's slave.

Today, Marco Pierre White is regarded as one of the most influential chefs in Britain (as well as the most foul-tempered, most mercurial, and most bullying), and it's an extraordinary fortuity that these two men, both in their early twenties, found themselves in a tiny pub kitchen together. Batali didn't understand what he was witnessing: his restaurant experience had been making strombolis in New Brunswick. "I assumed I was seeing what everyone else already knew. I didn't feel like I was on the cusp of a revolution. And yet, while I had no idea this guy was about to become so famous, I could see he was preparing food from outside the box. He was a genius on the plate. I'd never worked on presentation. I just put shit on the plate." He described White's making a deep green puree from basil leaves and then a white butter sauce, then swirling the green sauce in one direction, and the white sauce in the other, and drawing a swerving line down the middle of the plate. "I had never seen anyone draw fucking lines with two sauces." White would order Batali to follow him to market ("I was his whipping boy—'Yes, master,' I'd answer, 'whatever you say, master'") and they'd return with game birds or ingredients for some of the most improbable dishes ever to be served in an English pub: *écrevisses* in a reduced lobster sauce, oysters with caviar, roasted ortolan (a rare, tiny bird served virtually breathing, gulped down, innards and all, like a raw crustacean)—"the whole menu written out in fucking French."

According to Batali, White was basically illiterate, but because he was so intuitive and physical—"a beautiful specimen, perfect, a classic body, like a sculpture, with broad shoulders, narrow waist"—he could do things to food that no one else had done before. "He made a hollandaise by beating the sauce so vigorously that it began to froth up and became something else—it was like a sabayon." He was forever chopping things, reducing them, and making Batali force them through a sieve—"which was no bigger than a fucking tea strainer, because it was a pub and that was all he had, and I'd spend my whole day crushing some chunky shellfish reduction through this tiny thing, ramming it over and over again with a wooden spoon."

White's term of choice was "navvy." "You know, we're just two guys in the kitchen," Batali recalls, "and I'm not cooking the fries right, according to him, or the zucchini, or whatever it was, and he tells me to sauté the snow peas instead, while he's over in the corner doing some dramatic thing with six crayfish, and suddenly he calls out, 'Bring me the snow peas *now*,' and I duly bring them over. 'Here are the snow peas, master,' but he doesn't like the look of them. 'They're wrong, you arsehole. They're overcooked, you fucking moron. You've ruined them, you goddamn fucking navvy.' But I'm an American, and I didn't understand what 'navvy' meant, and I'd say something like 'Navvy this, navvy that, if you don't like my snow peas then make them yourself,' which made him even angrier." He threw a risotto into Batali's chest. He beat up an Irish kid who washed the dishes. "He was intimidating," Batali recalls. He stuck it out for four months—"I was frightened for my life, this guy was a mean motherfucker"—then dumped two handfuls of salt into a beurre blanc and walked out.

"I will never forget him," White said, when I met him in London. "He has fucking big calves, doesn't he? He should donate them to the kitchen when he dies. They'll make a great osso buco. If he walked in today, and I saw only those calves, I'd know it was Mario." According to White, Mario wasn't taking his calling seriously. "The sleeping thing killed him." He would have been a perfectly competent chef, White said, if only he'd got up when his alarm went off. He recalls dispatching Batali to buy tropical fruit. "He came back with four avocados. He was worn out. He didn't know what he was doing. He'd been out until four in the morning. He was wild. Hard core. Joy Division was his favorite band, and that says it all." White put his finger to his nose and sniffed. "Know what I mean?" White shook his head. "Would it be fair to say that, in those days, his enthusiasm for gastronomy was considerably greater than his talent? Is that a fair comment? Has his talent caught up?"

In White's kitchen, Batali was a failure, and you can tell that he'd like to dismiss the experience but can't: after all, White was the first person to show Batali what a chef could be. As a result, White is both loathed by Batali and respected. Even now, twenty years later, you hear in Batali's account a nagging irritation at his failure to charm or work with someone who understood so much about the potential of food—that "it was a wide-open game." From White, Batali learned the virtues of presentation, speed, stamina, and intense athletic cooking. And from White he acquired a hatred of things French. Batali has an injunction against reduced sauces, the business of boiling a meat broth until it is reduced to an intense syrup. ("If you can run your finger through it and it leaves an impression, then it's not me, we won't serve it, it's too French.") And a prohibition against tantrums. ("It's so old school, so made for the movies.") But mainly Batali learned how much he had to learn.

Provoked by White's command, Batali embarked on a grand tour of the grandest restaurants in Europe, tracing White's skills back to their origins like someone following a genealogical line: the Tour d'Argent in Paris; the Moulin de Mougins, in Provence; the Waterside Inn, outside London, then regarded as the best restaurant in Britain. "In four months, you learn the essentials of the place," Batali told me. "If you want to learn them properly, you have to stay a year, to cook through the seasons. But I was in a hurry." Most of the time, Batali was stuck doing highly repetitive tasks: squeezing duck carcasses, night after night, using a machine designed to get that extra ounce of juice to go into a duck stock, which, in turn, would be reduced into one of those "sticky, gummy" sauces for which Batali was developing such a distaste. "You learn by working in the kitchen. Not by reading a book or watching a television program or going to cooking school. That's how it's done."

That's what I wanted to do—to work in the Babbo kitchen, as Mario's slave.

"You learn by working in the kitchen," Mario Batali tells Bill Buford. "Not by reading a book or watching a television program or going to cooking school." Generate reasons and evidence to support this statement and to refute it. After you have considered different positions, which do you agree with? Why?

Buford uses *Heat*, from which "Dinner with Mario" is excerpted, to paint a distinctive profile of one of America's most famous chefs. Write a brief profile essay that reveals an important character trait of a person who works with food (the person doesn't have to be a professional). You should reveal something about your subject as you describe him or her cooking, serving or selling food, or doing whatever it is with food that the person does.

Excess best captures the spirit of Mario Batali in Buford's piece. The New York chef consumes not glasses but cases of wine; he feeds his fellow dinner guests multiple servings of pure fat; and he stuffs a rival chef with copious amounts of pig. "Wretched excess," Batali claims, "is just barely enough." As a group, think about the concept of excess as it relates to our cultural obsession with celebrities. What other famous (or infamous) artists, actors, athletes, musicians, or other media stars can you think of who revel in excess? How do they engage in and display their excesses? Do you see a link between the nature of celebrity and the need for these kinds of behaviors?

DINING OUT

The essays that open this book—from "The Cooking Ape," which considers the role of cooking in human evolution, to "Dinner with Mario," the memoir of a home cook who dreams of working in the kitchen of a world famous chef—have been, in one way or another, about *dining in*. That is, they have focused on the ways that food deeply connects with family, home, and the self, and we hope that they have helped you consider the power of food to shape individual identity.

The texts that follow, on the other hand—beginning with the menus you'll find on the next few pages—are all about *dining out*. They move away from the home and individual identity and expand outward, broadening our examination of food to include its role in culture, politics, and ideology.

It is these cultural, political, and ideological themes we'd like you to consider as you read and analyze the menus that follow. The menus, from Angelica Kitchen, a vegan café in the East Village of New York City, and Moe's Southwest Grill, a popular and lively burrito franchise often found in college towns, demonstrate the distinctive food philosophies of each restaurant. As you read, think of them as more than just a list of food items from which to choose when you're hungry for lunch. Think of them instead as the textual representations of the restaurants they represent. You should note that the menu for Moe's doesn't include prices because these differ by region.

A complete and effective menu is a sophisticated rhetorical document. It articulates the relationship the restaurant wants to establish with its guests, and it creates an ethos for the restaurant and the people who work there. As you read these menus, consider what they say about the restaurants themselves, their identities, their politics, and the experiences they promise their guests. We've included some research, invention, and writing prompts to help you accomplish this, and after you've spent some time thinking about the menus from Angelica Kitchen and Moe's Southwest Grill, you'll be ready to undertake Major Assignment 2—which asks you to analyze the menu of a restaurant in your area—on page 191.

Soups Starters & Sides

Miso Soup with wakame and tofu   cup 3.50   bowl 3.75

☀ **Soup of the day**   cup 3.50   bowl 4.25

Kombu Vegetable Bouillon   1.75
A warm invigorating cup of broth, rich in minerals, delicately seasoned with ginger, sage & thyme

Soba Sensation   6.50
Rich, velvety sesame sauce ladled over soba noodles, topped with pickled red cabbage garnish.

Curried Cashew Spread   4.75
An intriguing live blend of raw cashews, sprouted chickpeas, freshly ground curry powder & unpasteurized miso. Accompanied by crisp crudités.

Thai Mee Up   7.25
All Raw – delicate strands of daikon radish, zucchini & carrot dressed with Thai tahini sauce, garnished with garlic-lemon marinated kale.

Hummus   6.50
Served with baked zahtar pita wedges and crisp crudités.

☀ **Norimaki**   8.00
Six pieces of rolled vegetable sushi, served with wasabi, pickled ginger & lemon-shoyu dipping sauce. *(ingredients vary daily)*

Angelica Pickle Plate   4.25
Garlic pickled shiitakes, assorted seasonal pickled vegetables & marinated beets.

Kimchee   3.25
Homemade, mild style, tangy fermented cabbage with carrot, daikon & jalapeno pepper.

Ruby Kraut   2.75
Homemade red cabbage sauerkraut.

Walnut-Lentil Pâté   6.75
Topped with tofu sour cream, served with baked rice crackers and crisp crudités.

Mashed Yukon Gold Potatoes   4.75
Served with brown rice gravy

Special Appetizer Agrarian Salgado   8.00
Baked rounds of mashed Yukon Gold potatoes and herbed seitan, with a basil-walnut pesto center; topped with dill-tofu sour cream & garnished with piquant marinated kale.

Brazil's mass social movements are mobilizing forces to end hunger. A portion of the proceeds from this appetizer goes to FRIENDS OF THE BRAZILIAN LANDLESS WORKERS MOVEMENT (MST) to support their implementation of agrarian reform and widespread development of sustainable agriculture. Learn more by visiting www.mstbrazil.org

Union Square farmer's market

Beverages

Juices – Made to Order
   Carrot   5.00
   Carrot/apple   5.00
   Carrot/mixed vegetable   6.50
   added fresh ginger   .35

Lemonade – Vibrant!   2.75
Hibiscus Cooler   2.75
  – Chilled hibiscus flower served with lime
Apple Cider – Chilled   2.75
Grain Coffee with Rice Dream   2.50
   grain coffee refill   1.25

Chai – Black tea, chai spices & soymilk;   2.75
sweetened with agave nectar
   chai tea refill   1.50

Green Tea   1.75
Kukicha Tea   Hot/Chilled   1.25/1.50
Mu 16 Tea   1.50
   first tea refill free

☀ See the Special Today page for today's selections

Angelica Kitchen

Entrees

☀ Daily Seasonal Specials
Descriptions of today's selections listed on overleaf.
À la carte 15.25   With choice of two Basics or cup of soup   17.50

Dashi and Noodles
Bowl of traditional Japanese broth made with shiitake mushrooms, kombu, fresh ginger & shoyu; served warm or cool over soba noodles. Adorned with chef's select garnishes.

	small	8.50
	large	10.50

Three Bean Chili
Piquant chili made with homemade seitan, kidney and pinto beans & lentils; slowly simmered with sun-dried tomatoes and a blend of chiles; topped with lime-jalapeño tofu sour cream. Served with fluffy Southern style cornbread & cucumber-red onion salsa.

	wee	9.00
	grand	11.50

Olé Man Seitan
Homemade seitan & roasted vegetable mix folded into a warm whole wheat tortilla; dressed with spicy traditional mole sauce (peanuts & chocolate), & lime-jalapeño tofu sour cream; garnished with pimento.   14.50

Thai Mee Up
An All Raw Entree - delicate strands of daikon radish, zucchini & carrot, on a bed of garlic-lemon marinated kale, dressed with Thai tahini sauce.   11.25

☀ Norimaki
Nine pieces of rolled vegetable sushi, served with wasabi, pickled ginger & lemon-shoyu dipping sauce *(ingredients vary daily)*   11.50

Sandwiches

Wrapsody
Seasonal selection of roasted vegetables, balsamic marinated beets, creamy hummus, dill pickles, sunflower sprouts & arugula, folded & wrapped in a soft whole wheat tortilla.   10.50

Sam or I Sandwich
Herbed baked tofu layered with marinated hiziki & arame, crisp grated daikon, ruby kraut, a smear of mellow sesame spread & lettuce. Served on choice of mixed grain or spelt bread.   8.75
Half a sandwich with simple salad or cup of soup & kukicha tea. 9.50

Marinated Tofu Sandwich
Lemon herbed baked tofu layered with roasted vegetables, a smear of basil-walnut pesto & lettuce. Served on choice of mixed grain or spelt bread.   8.75
Half a sandwich with simple salad or cup of soup & kukicha tea. 9.50

Salads

House
Assorted lettuces; sunflower sprouts; grated red & green cabbage, daikon, carrots and beets; topped with clover sprouts; served with your choice of dressing.   7.50

Roasted Vegetable Salad
A seasonal selection of roasted vegetables tossed with arugula in a balsamic vinaigrette. Garnished with garlic crostini spread with creamy hummus, & cherry tomatoes.   12.75

Sea Caesar
Crisp romaine lettuce tossed with creamy garlic dressing. Topped with seasoned sourdough croutons, a sprinkle of smoked dulse & nori strips.   8.75

Orchard
Mesclun lettuces, apple, toasted pecans, dried bing cherries & sourdough croutons; tossed in a rosemary vinaigrette.   9.25

Mixed Sprout
A refreshing toss of snow pea shoots, sunflower sprouts & seeds, and mint; mixed with cabbage, daikon & carrots in a cool mint vinaigrette. Adorned with toasted peanuts, onion sprouts & watercress.   8.75

Si Se Puede
Balsamic roasted cherry tomatoes & basil-olive marinated chickpeas, over local greens tossed with extra virgin olive oil, fresh squeezed lemon juice & coarse sea salt. Accompanied by garlic crostini topped with tofu ricotta & chives.   10.00

Well Cultured
Mélange of seasonal greens & watercress tossed with homemade kimchee, nori strips, toasted sesame seeds & extra virgin olive oil; garnish of radish slices.   8.75

Tempeh Reuben Sandwich (served warm)
Our version of this classic features baked marinated tempeh, seasoned with caraway & cumin, tofu Russian dressing, sauerkraut & lettuce. Served on choice of mixed grain or spelt bread.   8.75
Half a sandwich with simple salad or cup of soup & kukicha tea. 9.50

Hot Open Face Tempeh Sandwich
Slices of sourdough baguette topped with lightly marinated & baked tempeh, napped with savory mushroom gravy. Served on a bed of raw spinach, garnished with ruby kraut.   10.50
With a scoop of mashed potatoes   11.50

 ☀ See the Special Today page for today's selections

Angelica Kitchen

Dragon Bowls

Part of the Angelica Kitchen menu since day one, this special combination of Basics is named for the Chinese bowl in which it was originally served.
(one substitution only)

Dragon Bowl   13.00
Rice, beans, tofu, sea vegetables & steamed vegetables; served with your choice of dressing.

Dragon Bargain   18.00
A Dragon Bowl served with cup of soup and bread with spread.

Wee Dragon   9.00
A Dragon Bowl in half portion.

Wee Dragon Bargain   14.00
A half Dragon served with cup of soup and bread with spread.

Combo Bowls

Any combination of the Basics at right served with your choice of dressing

choice of 2	7.25
choice of 3	9.50
choice of 4	11.00

Dressings & Sauces

House – Puree of tahini, scallions & parsley
Tangy Basil – Sweet & sour, oil free
Black Sesame – with wasabi, garlic & toasted sesame oil
Balsamic Vinaigrette – Balsamic vinegar, olive oil & mustard
Creamy Carrot – with ginger & dill
Brown Rice Gravy – Brown rice flour roux with a savory blend of herbs, spices & tamari

Refills are .95 on all dressings above

Soba Sensation Sauce – Rich, velvety sesame sauce	1.90
Sea Caesar Dressing – Creamy garlic dressing	1.90

Angelica Kitchen Organic Brittle
Ingredients: pumpkin seeds, sunflower seeds, sesame seeds, pecans, rice syrup, maple sugar, vanilla, sea salt.

Packaged To Go.

small 1.1 oz	2.75
large 3.2 oz	6.75

☀ See the Special Today page for today's selections

Picnic Plate

Select menu items, served cool, to mix & match.
*starred items available in larger à la carte portions elsewhere on menu.

3 items	7.75
4 items	9.50
5 items	11.50

Assorted Seasonal Pickled Vegetables*	Baked Marinated Tofu
Walnut-Lentil Pâté*	Today's Special Vegetable
Norimaki* *(two pieces)*	Marinated Hiziki & Arame Salad
Simple Salad*	Baked Marinated Tempeh
Hummus*	Today's Salad Special*
Ruby Kraut*	Live Curried Cashew Spread*
Kimchee*	Garlic Lemon Marinated Kale

Basics

Served with your choice of dressing

Tofu	3.75
Tempeh	4.25
Beans	3.00
Sea Vegetables	4.25
Steamed Vegetables	4.00
Simple Salad	5.50
Soba Noodles	3.75
Rice	2.75
Millet	3.50
3 Grain Mix	3.75
(quinoa, teff & amaranth)	

Breads & Spreads

Angelica Cornbread
Rustic, whole grain slice (wheat free)   2.00

Sourdough Bread
Authentic tangy whole wheat slice   1.75

Southern Style Cornbread
Generous square, light & fluffy (wheat)   3.25

Small Angelica Cornbread Loaf   7.50

Miso-Tahini Spread
Rich & smooth   2.00

Ginger-Carrot Spread
Light & bright   1.75

Onion Spread
Sweet & savory   1.75

glossary

Agar
Marine algae used as a vegetarian gelling agent.

Amaranth
Tiny golden seeds, extraordinarily nutritious, amaranth was once the sacred food of the Aztecs. Cooked as a grain, it has the aroma of fresh corn & the crunch & appearance of blonde caviar. Higher than milk in protein & calcium.

Arame *(AHR-ah-may)*
Dark brown sea vegetable, thin & thread-like, with a mild, sweet taste; rich in iron, calcium & iodine.

Burdock
A slender root vegetable with a sweet, earthy flavor & a tender crisp texture. Acts as a blood purifier & is an excellent source of potassium

Daikon *(DI-kon)*
Large white radish; mild, pungent & crisp with remarkable medicinal qualities.

Dulse
Reddish purple sea vegetable, often an immediate favorite of those first tasting seaweed. High in iron & protein, our dulse is harvested from the coast of Maine.

Gomasio
A low sodium table condiment consisting of dry roasted, crushed sesame seeds & sea salt

Grain Coffee
Caffeine free beverage made from roasted barley, rye, chicory & roots

Hiziki *(hijiki)*
A dark brown sea vegetable with a strong flavor of the ocean. Resembling thin black spaghetti, hiziki is the most mineral rich of all foods & is considered by the Japanese as "esteemed beauty food"

Kamut *(Kah-MOOT)*
Heirloom durum wheat, plump, golden & high in protein & minerals. Many people allergic to common wheat find kamut easier to digest.

Kanten
Light, soothing gelled dessert made with apple cider, agar & fruit

Kombu
Wide, thick, dark green sea vegetable, very high in vitamins A & C as well as potassium & calcium. Useful as a natural flavor & health enhancer.

Kukicha Tea
A satisfying cup with body & deep flavor, made from the roasted twigs of the tea plant. A digestive aid, "twig tea" has less than one quarter of the caffeine content of black tea.

Millet
A gluten-free small yellow grain with a nutty flavor, easy to digest & having a rich amino acid profile, millet is among the earliest cultivated grains.

Mirin
Ambrosial cooking wine, naturally brewed & fermented from sweet brown rice.

Miso
A protein-rich fermented paste made from soybeans, sea salt, koji & a grain; sweet & light to deep & hearty in taste depending on the grain used & the aging time. An invaluable digestive aid, miso is also known for reducing the effects of environmental pollution.

Mu 16 Tea
A distinctive combination of 16 plants & herbs with a natural sweetness from licorice root. Delicate, full-bodied & caffeine free, Mu tea is good for relieving tiredness.

Nori
Thin black or dark green crisp sheets of dried sea vegetable, with a delicate nutlike flavor & a fresh sea essence. Remarkably, nori contains more vitamin A than carrots & is 35.6% protein.

Quinoa *(KEEN-wha)*
A staple of the ancient Incas, who called it the Mother Grain, quinoa is light & fluffy & the highest source of protein of any grain.

Sea Palm
Domestic brown sea vegetable, mildly sweet with a pleasing al dente texture. Helps reduce cholesterol & supports normal thyroid function.

Seitan *(SAY-tan)*
Made from whole wheat flour, seitan is concentrated wheat protein. Succulent & chewy, it takes on the flavor of other ingredients with which it is cooked. At Angelica's, we make our own here, fresh on the premises.

Shoyu
Fermented nutritious flavor enhancer made from whole soybeans, salt, water & wheat koji. Shoyu provides richer seasoning with less salt, containing 1/7 the amount of sodium as plain salt.

Soba
Tan Japanese noodles made of buckwheat or a blend of buckwheat & whole wheat.

Spelt
An ancient red wheat. People with sensitivities to wheat often have a better tolerance for spelt because it contains a unique form of gluten that is easier to digest.

Tahini
Smooth, creamy high-protein paste made from hulled ground sesame seeds.

Teff
Tiny grain with giant nutritional superiority. Having a pleasing nutty flavor, teff boasts 12% protein & is especially high in calcium & iron.

Tempeh
A traditional Indonesian soy food, exceptionally high in protein; made into a firm cake from soybeans, water & special culture. One of the plant kingdom's richest sources of vitamin B12.

Tofu
Soybean curd made from fresh soymilk, then pressed into blocks. Fresh Tofu in Pennsylvania produces Angelica's tofu from non-hybridized New York State organically grown soybeans.

Udon
A light flat Japanese wheat noodle.

Umeboshi *(Ume)*
Salty, refreshingly sour, pickled plums that stimulate the appetite & enhance digestion.

Wakame
Long thin green sea vegetable with sweet taste & delicate texture. High in calcium & rich in iodine.

Rebecca Wood's <u>The New Whole Foods Encyclopedia</u> has been a great resource in compiling this glossary.

We Happily Accept only cash

The Angelica Home Kitchen cookbook is available for purchase.

Gift Certificates Available

Gratuities will be added to parties of 6 or more.

www.angelicakitchen.com

Illustration at left by Tom Donald   Inside illustrations by Flavia Bacarella
Cover photograph by John Bigelow Taylor

Angelica Kitchen

All burritos, tacos and quesadillas come with your choice of black or pinto beans, choice of grilled sirloin steak, chicken, pulled pork, ground beef or tofu.

Chips and salsa free with every meal!

BURRITOS

Original   Junior

homewrecker
Choice of grilled meat, beans, rice, shredded cheese, pico de gallo, lettuce, sour cream and guacamole

triple lindy
Choice of grilled meat, beans, rice, shredded cheese, pico de gallo and guacamole or sour cream

joey bag of donuts
Choice of grilled meat, beans, rice, shredded cheese and pico de gallo

art vandalay
Beans, rice, shredded cheese, pico de gallo, lettuce, sour cream and guacamole (vegetarian)

Be a Streaker! Lose the tortilla!

RICE BOWLS

tofu bowl
Rice, black beans, tofu, grilled mushrooms, grilled onions, pico de gallo, cheese, cucumbers, olives

chicken bowl
Rice, pinto beans, grilled chicken, grilled peppers, grilled mushrooms, pico de gallo, cheese, spicy chipotle ranch

pork bowl
Rice, pinto beans, pork, grilled onions, pico de gallo, cheese, queso, cilantro

MAKE IT A MEAL

Add a regular drink and a side of queso or guacamole to any entrée

ADD-ONS

extra steak or pork
extra meat
bacon
queso
guacamole

grilled veggies
sautéed mushrooms
sour cream
pico de gallo

TACOS
Served with hard or soft shells

overachiever
Choice of grilled meat, beans, shredded cheese, pico de gallo, lettuce, sour cream and guacamole

unanimous decision
Beans, shredded cheese, pico de gallo, lettuce, sour cream and guacamole (vegetarian)

the funk meister
Choice of grilled meat, beans, shredded cheese, pico de gallo and lettuce

QUESADILLAS

john coctostan
Choice of grilled meat, beans and shredded cheese with a side of pico de gallo and sour cream

instant friend
Beans, shredded cheese and sautéed veggies with a side of pico de gallo and sour cream (vegetarian)

super kingpin
Shredded cheese with a side of pico de gallo and sour cream (vegetarian)

SALADS
All salads served with choice of dressing

close talker
Lettuce, choice of grilled meat, beans, shredded cheese, pico de gallo, cucumbers and black olives

personal trainer
Lettuce, beans, shredded cheese, pico de gallo, cucumbers and black olives (vegetarian)

FAJITAS
Served with three flour tortillas

fat sam
Choice of grilled meat, peppers & onions, shredded cheese, pico de gallo, lettuce, sour cream and guacamole

alfredo garcia
Choice of grilled meat, peppers & onions, shredded cheese, pico de gallo and lettuce

Moe's Southwest Grill

NACHOS

billy barou
Choice of grilled meat, beans, queso, pico de gallo, jalapeños and black olives

ruprict
Beans, queso, pico de gallo, jalapeños and black olives (vegetarian)

KIDS MENU

(12 and under) Includes cookie and beverage

moo moo mr cow
Kid-sized burrito with choice of grilled meat, beans, rice, shredded cheese and pico de gallo

power wagon
Hard or soft taco with choice of grilled meat, shredded cheese and lettuce

mini masterpiece
Kid-sized cheese quesadilla with a side of pico de gallo and sour cream

QUESO, GUAC & SIDES

queso	Cup	Bowl
guacamole	Cup	Bowl
pico de gallo	Cup	Bowl
rice	Cup	Bowl
beans	Cup	Bowl
chocolate chip cookie	Cup	Bowl
oatmeal raisin cookie	Cup	Bowl

BEVERAGES

medium/large

Coca-Cola fountain drinks
iced tea
bottled water

CATERING MENU

Minimum order required for delivery
Additional charge for steak or pork may apply

FAJITA BAR

2 flour tortillas, Choice of: Chicken, Pulled Pork*, Sirloin Steak*, Ground Beef or Tofu, Rice and Beans, Onions (by request), Peppers (by request), Shredded Cheese, Shredded Lettuce, Sour Cream, Guacamole, Pico de Gallo, Chips & Salsa.

SALAD BAR

Crispy Salad Shells, Shredded Lettuce, Choice of: Chicken, Pulled Pork*, Sirloin Steak*, Ground Beef or Tofu, Pinto or Black Beans, Shredded Cheese, Pico de Gallo, Cucumbers, Olives, Dressings, Chips & Salsa.

TACO BAR

Soft flour tortillas and/or crispy corn shells, Choice of: Chicken, Pulled Pork*, Sirloin Steak*, Ground Beef or Tofu, Pinto or Black Beans, Shredded Cheese, Shredded Lettuce, Pico de Gallo, Chips & Salsa.

DIPS

All dips priced by the 12 oz. bowl. Feeds 3-4 people.

Sour Cream

Guacamole

Moe's Queso

Pico De Gallo

Additional Salsas

Prices may vary by location.

Moe's Southwest Grill

MINI BURRITO APPETIZER

A miniature version of our famous pre-rolled burritos with the following ingredients; Flour tortilla, Rice, Beans, Choice of: Chicken, Pulled Pork*, Sirloin Steak*, Ground Beef or Tofu, Pico De Gallo, Shredded Cheese, Chips and Salsa.

BOX O' BURRITOS

One of our famous pre-rolled burritos with the following ingredients: Flour tortilla, Rice and Beans, Choice of: Chicken, Pulled Pork*, Sirloin Steak*, Ground Beef or Tofu, Pico De Gallo, Shredded Cheese, Chips and Salsa.

MAKE IT A MEAL

Coca-Cola products

call us today to place your order

FREE CHIPS & SALSA WITH EVERY ORDER!

seven signs that You're seeing in Moe-Vision

1. You yell "Welcome to Moe's®" along with the crew

2. You never pay for chips and salsa

3. You sell your microwave on ebay®

4. Your iPod® is filled with songs from the dearly departed

5. You start naming everything you eat after an inside joke

6. There is a four-way tie for the clean plate award

7. You campaign for queso to become its own food group

Moe's Southwest Grill

Explore

In the preceding pages, you'll find the menus from Angelica Kitchen (*http://www.angelicakitchen.com/*) and Moe's Southwest Grill (*http://www.moes.com/*). Using the restaurants' home pages, as well as other publications that have written about them (use the web page links and your library's databases to find these), gather some background about these two businesses. Use the information you've found to write up a brief profile of each restaurant and note the key similarities and differences you find. Remember to properly cite your sources. As you conduct your research, consider the following questions:

- How long have the companies been in business?

- What kind of business model does each restaurant have?

- What are the respective corporate missions?

- What kinds of advertising does each restaurant use? What kinds of affiliated merchandise do they sell?

- Who is the target demographic for each restaurant?

- What kinds of notices have the restaurants received?

- How do the restaurants seem to interact with their surrounding communities?

Collaborate

As part of a small group, develop a new menu item for either Angelica Kitchen or Moe's Southwest Grill. The item you propose should fit with the restaurant's overall image and food philosophy. (For example, it wouldn't make any sense to propose a rare fillet of beef for Angelica Kitchen given their organic, vegan mission.) After you've decided on your dish, write an appropriate name and menu description, and think about how you would propose this to the restaurant owner for inclusion on the menu. You might need to consult some cookbooks or websites to come up with your dish, but have some fun and be creative. Take this chance to fill a gap in a menu or to propose something you'd really like to eat.

As practice for Major Assignment 2 (on page 191), choose either the menu from Angelica Kitchen or from Moe's Southwest Grill and write a brief descriptive analysis of the restaurant's food and eating philosophy as they emerge from the menu's words, images, and document design. To generate ideas for your analysis, consider the following questions:

- How would you describe the menu as a visual document? Think, for example, about typography, including font selection; the kind, use and placement of images; and the use of space. Consider how each of these elements works separately and how they come together as a whole to produce a rhetorical effect.

- How is the menu organized? What kind of food narrative does it create?

- How does the menu try to connect with its customers? Think about the level or formality, about diction—including the names given to items on the menu—pop culture allusions, as well as appeals to the customers' emotions and intellect.

- Based on reading the menu, what kind of dining experience do you expect when you got to this restaurant?

- What is the restaurant's ethos? In other words, how does the restaurant want to be perceived by its customers? And what does the menu do to convey this corporate persona?

- What is the restaurant's food philosophy or mission? Think about the actual food items the restaurant prepares and sells and about how the menu names and describes these items.

Classically trained chef Anthony Bourdain also writes books and appears on television—as the star of the Travel Channel's "No Reservations" and as a guest judge on Bravo's "Top Chef." "Who Cooks?" and "Food is Good" (which starts on page 63) are excerpts from his 2000 book Kitchen Confidential: Adventures in the Culinary Underbelly. In "Who Cooks?" Bourdain writes about the people who work in restaurant kitchens and makes some interesting observations about food and gender. That subject comes up in several pieces through this book, including the two that follow this one, "A Woman's Place?" and "What's that Smell in the Kitchen?" Writing prompts for this excerpt follow "A Woman's Place?"

WHO COOKS?

By Anthony Bourdain

Who's cooking your food anyway? What strange beasts lurk behind the kitchen doors? You see the chef: he's the guy without the hat, with the clipboard under his arm, maybe his name stitched in Tuscan blue on his starched white chef's coat next to those cotton Chinese buttons. But who's actually cooking your food? Are they young, ambitious culinary school grads, putting in their time on the line until they get their shot at the Big Job? Probably not. If the chef is anything like me, the cooks are a dysfunctional, mercenary lot, fringe-dwellers motivated by money, the peculiar lifestyle of cooking and a grim pride. They're probably not even American.

Line cooking done well is a beautiful thing to watch. It's a high-speed collaboration resembling, at its best, ballet or modern dance. A properly organized, fully loaded line cook, one who works clean, and has "moves"—meaning economy of movement, nice technique and, most important, speed—can perform his duties with Nijinsky-like grace. The job requires character—and endurance. A good line cook never shows up late, never calls in sick, and works through pain and injury.

What most people don't get about professional-level cooking is that it is not at all about the best recipe, the most innovative presentation, the most creative marriage of ingredients, flavors and textures; that, presumably, was all arranged long before you sat down to dinner. Line cooking—the real business of preparing the food you eat—is more about consistency, about mindless, unvarying repetition, the same series of tasks performed over and over and over again in exactly the same way. The last thing a chef wants in a line cook is an innovator, somebody with ideas of his own who is going to mess around with the chef's recipes and presentations. Chefs require blind, near-fanatical loyalty, a strong back and an automaton-like consistency of execution under battlefield conditions.

A three-star Italian chef pal of mine was recently talking about why he—a proud Tuscan who makes his own pasta and sauces from scratch daily and runs one of the best restaurant kitchens in New York—would never be so foolish as to hire any Italians to cook on his line. He greatly prefers Ecuadorians, as many chefs do: 'The Italian guy? You screaming at him in the rush, "Where's that risotto? Is that fucking risotto ready yet? Gimme that risotto!" . . . and the Italian . . . he's gonna *give it to you* . . . An Ecuadorian guy? He's gonna just turn his back . . . and stir the risotto and keep cooking it *until it's done the way you showed him.* That's what I want.'

I knew just what he meant. Generally speaking, American cooks—meaning, born in the USA, possibly school-trained, culinarily sophisticated types who know before you show them what *monter au beurre* means and how to make a béarnaise sauce—are a lazy, undisciplined and, worst of all, high-maintenance lot, annoyingly opinionated, possessed of egos requiring constant stroking and tune-ups, and, as members of a privileged and wealthy population, unused to the kind of "disrespect" a busy chef is inclined to dish out. No one understands and appreciates the American Dream of hard work leading to material rewards better than a non-American. The Ecuadorian, Mexican, Dominican and Salvadorian cooks I've worked with over the years make most CIA-educated white boys look like clumsy, sniveling little punks.

In New York City, the days of the downtrodden, underpaid illegal immigrant cook, exploited by his cruel masters, have largely passed—at least where quality line cooks are concerned. Most of the Ecuadorians and Mexicans I hire from a large pool—a sort of farm team of associated and often related former dishwashers—are very well-paid professionals, much sought after by other chefs. Chances are they've worked their way up from the bottom rung; they remember well what it was like to empty out grease traps, scrape plates, haul leaking bags of garbage out to the curb at four o' clock in the morning. A guy who's come up through the ranks, who knows every station, every recipe, every corner of the restaurant and who has learned, first and foremost, *your* system above all others is likely to be more valuable and long-term than some bed-wetting white boy whose mom brought him up thinking the world owed him a living, and who thinks he actually knows a few things.

You want loyalty from your line cooks. Somebody who wakes up with a scratchy throat and slight fever and thinks it's okay to call in sick is not what I'm looking for. While it's necessary for cooks to take pride in their work—it's a good idea to let a good cook stretch a little now and again with the occasional contribution of a special or a soup—this is still the army. Ultimately, I want a salute and a 'Yes, sir!' If I want an opinion from my line cooks, *I'll* provide one. Your customers arrive expecting the same dish prepared the same way they had it before; they don't want some budding Wolfgang Puck having fun with kiwis and coriander with a menu item they've come to love.

There are plenty of exceptions, of course. I have a few Americans in my traveling road show, a few key people whom I tend to hire over and over as I move from place to place. The relationship between chef and sous-chef can be a particularly intimate one, for instance, and it's nice to have someone with a similar background and world-view when you're going to spend almost every waking hour together. Women line cooks, however rare they might be in the testosterone-heavy, male-dominated world of restaurant kitchens, are a particular delight. To have a tough-as-nails, foul-mouthed, trash-talking female line cook on your team can be a true joy—and a civilizing factor in a unit where conversation tends to center around who's got the bigger balls and who takes it in the ass.

I've been fortunate enough to work with some really studly women line cooks— no weak reeds these. One woman, Sharon, managed to hold down a busy sauté station while seven months pregnant—and still find time to provide advice and comfort to a romantically unhappy broiler man. A long-time associate, Beth, who likes to refer to herself as the 'Grill Bitch,' excelled at putting loudmouths and fools into their proper place. She refused to behave any differently than her male co-workers: she'd change in the same locker area, dropping her pants right alongside them. She was as sexually aggressive, and as vocal about it, as her fellow cooks, but unlikely to suffer behavior she found demeaning. One sorry Moroccan cook who pinched her ass found himself suddenly bent over a cutting board with Beth dry-humping him from behind, saying 'How do *you* like it, bitch?' The guy almost died of shame—and never repeated that mistake again.

Another female line cook I had the pleasure of working with arrived at work one morning to find that an Ecuadorian pasta cook had decorated her station with some particularly ugly hard-core pornography of pimply-assed women getting penetrated in every orifice by pot-bellied guys with prison tattoos and back hair. She didn't react at all, but a little later, while passing through the pasta man's station, casually remarked, "José, I see you brought in some photos of the family. Mom looks good for her age."

Mise-en-place is the religion of all good line cooks. Do *not* fuck with a line cook's "meez"—meaning their set-up, their carefully arranged supplies of sea salt, rough-cracked pepper, softened butter, cooking oil, wine, back-ups and so on. As a cook, your station, and its condition, its state of readiness, is an extension of your nervous system—and it is profoundly upsetting if another cook or, God forbid, a *waiter*—disturbs your precisely and carefully laid-out system. The universe is in order when your station is set up the way you like it: you know where to find everything with your eyes closed, everything you need during the course of the shift is at the ready at arm's reach, your defenses are deployed. If you let your mise-en-place run down, get dirty and disorganized, you'll quickly find yourself spinning in place and calling for back-up. I worked with a chef who used to step behind the line to a dirty cook's station in the middle of the rush to explain why the offending cook was falling behind. He'd press his palm down on the cutting board, which was littered with peppercorns, spattered sauce, bits of parsley, breadcrumbs, and the usual flotsam and jetsam that accumulates quickly on a station if not constantly wiped away with a moist side-towel. "You see this?" he'd inquire, raising his palm so that the cook could see the bits of dirt and scraps sticking to his chef's palm, "That's what the inside of your head looks like now. *Work clean!*"

Working clean, constantly wiping and cleaning, is a desirable state of affairs for the conscientious line cook. That chef was right: messy station equals messy mind. This explains why side-towels are hoarded like gold by good line cooks. When the linen order arrives, the smart cookies fall onto it voraciously, stashing stacks of the valuable objects anywhere they can hide them. One cook I knew would load them above the acoustic tile in the ceiling above his station, along with his favorite tongs, favorite non-stick pans, slotted spoons, and anything else he figured he needed on his station and didn't want another cook to get. I'm sure that years later, though that restaurant has changed hands many times since, future generations of cooks are still finding stashes of fluffy, clean side-towels.

It's not just clean that you value in a side-towel—it's *dry*. It's nice, wiping the rim of a plate with a slightly moist one, but try grabbing a red-hot sauté pan handle with a wet towel, and you'll learn fast why a fresh stack of dry towels is a necessity. Some traditional European kitchens still issue two towels per cook at the beginning of the shift: one to work with while the other dries on the oven handle. This strikes me as criminally parsimonious. I like a tall stack, conveniently located over my station, in neatly folded, kitty-cornered, easy-to-grab fashion, and I don't ever want to run out. I'll rip through twenty of them in the course of an eight-hour service period, and if it costs my masters a few bucks extra, tough. I'm not burning my hand or wiping grease on my nice plates because they're too mean to shell out for a few more rented towels.

What exactly is this mystical mise-en-place I keep going on about? Why are some line cooks driven to apoplexy at the pinching of even a few grains of salt, a pinch of parsley? Because it's *ours*. Because we set it up the way we want it. Because it's like our knives, about which you hear the comment: 'Don't touch my dick, *don't touch my knife.*'

A fairly standard mise-en-place is a pretty extensive list. A typical one would be composed of, for instance:

kosher or sea salt

crushed black peppercorns (hand-crushed—*not* ground in the blender)

ground white pepper

fresh breadcrumbs

chiffonade parsley

blended oil in wine bottle with speed pourer

extra virgin olive oil

white wine

brandy

chervil tops in ice water for garnish

chive sticks or chopped chives

tomato concasseé

caramelized apple sections

garlic confit

chopped or slivered garlic

chopped shallots

softened butter

favorite ladles, spoons, tongs, pans, pots, all sauces, portioned fish, meat, menu items, specials and back-ups conveniently positioned for easy access

Being set up properly, trained and coordinated is not nearly enough. A good line cook has to be able to remain clear-headed, organized and reasonably even-keeled during hectic and stressful service periods. When you've got thirty or forty or more tables all sitting down at the same time and ordering different items with different temperatures, the stuff has to come up together; the various stations— sauté, garde-manger, broiler, middle—have to assemble a party of ten's dinner at the same moment. You can't have one member of a party's Dover sole festering in the window by the sauté station while the grill guy waits for a rack of lamb to hit medium-rare. It's got to come up together! Your hero line cook doesn't let the screaming, the frantic cries of 'Is it ready yet?', the long and potentially confusing list of donenesses all working at the same time throw him. He's got to keep all those temperatures straight in his head, remembering which steak goes with what. He's got to be able to tune out the howls of outrage from the chef, the tiny, gibbering annoyances from the floor, the curses and questions and prompts from his co-workers: "Ready on seven? *Via*! Let's go! *Vamos*! Coming up on *seven*!"

The ability to 'work well with others' is a must. If you're a sauté man, your grill man is your dance partner, and chances are, you're spending the majority of your time working in a hot, uncomfortably confined, submarine-like space with him. You're both working around open flame, boiling liquids with plenty of blunt objects at close hand—and you both carry knives, lots of knives. So you had better get along. It will not do to have two heavily armed cooks duking it out behind the line over some perceived insult when there are vats of boiling grease and razor-sharp cutlery all around.

So who the hell, exactly, *are* these guys, the boys and girls in the trenches? You might get the impression from the specifics of *my* less than stellar career that all line cooks are wacked-out moral degenerates, dope fiends, refugees, a thuggish assortment of drunks, sneak thieves, sluts and psychopaths. You wouldn't be too far off base. The business, as respected three-star chef Scott Bryan explains it, attracts 'fringe elements,' people for whom something in their lives has gone terribly wrong. Maybe they didn't make it through high school, maybe they're running away from something—be it an ex-wife, a rotten family history, trouble with the law, a squalid Third World backwater with no opportunity for advancement. Or maybe, like me, they just like it here. They're comfortable with the rather relaxed and informal code of conduct in the kitchen, the elevated level of tolerance for eccentricity, unseemly personal habits, lack of documentation, prison experience. In most kitchens, one's freakish personal proclivities matter little if at all. Can you keep up? Are you ready for service? Can I count on you to show up at work tomorrow, to not let the side down?

That's what counts.

I can break down line cooks into three subgroups.

You've got your Artists: the annoying, high-maintenance minority. This group includes specialists like pâtissiers (the neurologists of cooking), sous-chefs, butchers, garde-manger psychos, the occasional saucier whose sauces are so ethereal and perfect that delusions of grandeur are tolerated.

Then there are the Exiles: people who just can't make it in any other business, could never survive a nine-to-five job, wear a tie or blend in with civilized society—and their comrades, the Refugees, usually émigrés and immigrants for whom cooking is preferable to death squads, poverty or working in a sneaker factory for 2 dollars a week.

Finally, there are the Mercenaries: people who do it for cash and do it well. Cooks who, though they have little love or natural proclivity for cuisine, do it at a high level because they are paid well to do it—and because they are professionals. Cooking is a *craft*, I like to think, and a good cook is a craftsman—*not* an artist. There's nothing wrong with that: the great cathedrals of Europe were built by craftsmen—though not designed by them. Practicing your craft in expert fashion is noble, honorable and satisfying. And I'll generally take a stand-up mercenary who takes pride in his professionalism over an artist any day. When I hear 'artist,' I think of someone who doesn't think it necessary to show up at work on time. More often than not their efforts, convinced as they are of their own genius, are geared more to giving themselves a hard-on than satisfying the great majority of dinner customers. Personally, I'd prefer to eat food that tastes good and is an honest reflection of its ingredients, than a 3-foot-tall caprice constructed from lemon grass, lawn trimmings, coconuts and red curry. You could lose an eye trying to eat that. When a job applicant starts telling me how Pacific Rim-job cuisine turns him on and inspires him, I see trouble coming. Send me another Mexican dishwasher anytime. I can teach *him* to cook. I *can't* teach character. Show up at work on time six months in a row and we'll talk about red curry paste and lemon grass. Until then, I have four words for you: "Shut the fuck up."

"What most people don't get about professional-level cooking," Anthony Bourdain writes, "is that it is not at all about the best recipe, the most innovative presentation, the most creative marriage of ingredients, flavors and textures; that, presumably, was all arranged long before you sat down to dinner. Line cooking—the real business of preparing the food you eat—is more about consistency, about mindless, unvarying repetition …"

As Anthony Bourdain points out in "Who Cooks?" women line cooks are uncommon in the "testosterone-heavy, male-dominated world of restaurant kitchens." And women chefs at top-flight restaurants are even rarer. In the following piece from October 2007, New York Magazine asked seven experts why "precious few women run New York kitchens."

A WOMAN'S PLACE?

By New York Magazine

We live in a golden age of chefs. Between your Batalis and Bouluds, your Vongerichtens and Riperts, your Masas and Morimotos, New York is bubbling over with cooking legends who not only practice world-class gastronomy but also manage to turn themselves into global gajillion-dollar megabrands. So here's a question: Where are all the women? Despite the fact that women make up the vast majority of home cooks, and despite four-plus decades of modern feminism, women still run just a small percentage of top kitchens in New York and elsewhere. Never mind the Rachael Rays and Nigella Lawsons of the world. They're TV personalities, not chefs. They don't turn out hundreds of meals a night on a hot, high-stress line at one of the country's most esteemed and critically scrutinized restaurants.

To explore why so few women reign over the city's leading culinary temples, we talked to seven prominent exceptions: April Bloomfield (The Spotted Pig), Rebecca Charles (Pearl Oyster Bar), Alex Guarnaschelli (Butter), Sara Jenkins (formerly of 50 Carmine), Anita Lo (Annisa), Jody Williams (Morandi), and Patricia Yeo (formerly of Monkey Bar and Sapa). It's worth noting that almost to a woman, the chefs we spoke to were at first reluctant to cite sexism as the reason there aren't more women among the city's elite chefs. In part, it seemed, they didn't want to play the victim or be labeled whiny; in part, they didn't want to believe it—the better to not let it stop them. "There are also a lot of men who can't hack it in the kitchen," was a common sentiment. But the more the women talked, the more it became clear that gender bias is still an issue.

Not that they don't embrace a stereotype or two themselves. The one thing the group agreed women do better than men? As Guarnaschelli put it: "Clean."

What did you make of the most recent "Top Chef" finale? This is the show's third season, and still, no woman has won. Why did Casey, the only woman in the finals, lose?

Rebecca Charles: Man, she had it in her hands. She had it! But she threw it away in the final round; her dishes just weren't good enough.

The fact that she's a woman had nothing to do with it?

Alex Guarnaschelli: I think the judges actually wanted her to win. I thought she would win. I'd chalk it up to an off day. That small thing—having a crap day—broke her chance. It didn't mean so much to me that she didn't win. I think she shattered the glass ceiling anyway.

Why aren't there more women chefs in New York? Is it harder to raise money as a woman?

Anita Lo: I kind of get the feeling that there are boys out there who have people running after them giving them money.

Patricia Yeo: Because they play golf together or they play poker together. Maybe we should go play poker with them, I don't know.

RC: It's the boys' club. It's incredible, and I never used to buy into stuff like that.

AG: I have colleagues—male colleagues—who say to me, "Yeah, I just met with a big group of investors to open a restaurant." I'm looking at them, trying to sip my coffee, like, "Yeah, bro, that must be rough." And I go home and trade in the coffee for tequila. Did I do something wrong?

Why don't women get the money?

PY: I think men aren't as nervous about asking. They seem to be able to say, "Listen, this is what I want, give it to me." Women, I think, have a harder time with it.

RC: Women are more unsure of themselves, no question, especially in terms of asking for money.

Sara Jenkins: It's like a pride thing, too; you fought so hard to be in a certain place. And now to have to turn around and say, "Oh, but wait, excuse me, I need a million dollars, please."

RC: Also, I've found that landlords will listen politely and then lease their space to a man with a track record. I had a long track record at the time I started Pearl Oyster Bar—twenty years as a chef, but not as a business owner. And that was the kind of track record they were looking for. I was lucky to find the guy that I found.

There must be some women-friendly investors out there.

RC: I do think there are businessmen in town that are women-friendly. But it's because they see women as, well, I hate to say this, but as a gimmick.

Jody Williams: And that doesn't mean they'll listen to them or give them a real role.

PY: But it's a double-edged sword; you get notoriety because you're a woman, but do you really want the notoriety because you're a woman? You want to be known just because you are a great chef.

What else keeps women from running kitchens?

RC: Some women seem to say that it's too hot, it's too much work. You have to give up a lot. That's what's hard for a lot of young women to understand. There are very few women who can have children and continue to operate restaurants, whether they're owners or chefs.

Are there "women's jobs" in professional kitchens?

RC: Pastry chef has always been the traditional one, and I think that's still true today.

April Bloomfield: It's an easy option for the girls to go into pastry.

RC: You're not on the hot line.

SJ: You don't have to compete with everybody else.

Is there a media bias against women chefs? Is it harder for women to get their names out there?

AG: You have to put on a pair of fishnet stockings, and you have to get yourself on television. I find myself hoping I can get on a TV show and then people from Oklahoma will come to my restaurant. Then I'll be able to make enough money to open my own place.

JW: If you're over-enthusiastic, though, you're a schoolgirl. I think that was printed about me.

Professional kitchens are traditionally shamelessly sexist. Is that still true?

AG: I worked in Paris for five years for Guy Savoy. And then one of the chefs was like, "You suck, you're a girl, I hate you." All the classic stereotypes. And Guy Savoy was like, "Will you just stop that crap and let her do her job? Let her cook the damn bass." And then when I burned it, Guy was like, "Ahh!" But he still believed in me.

AB: I didn't want the fact that I was a woman to be an issue, so I just put my head down and cooked and did the best that I could. I moved to wherever I was able to move. And one day, some guys came in and shook everyone's hands, and I held out my hand and this guy just walked straight past me. It's like, "Okay, fuck you. I'm gonna be better than you one day."

RC: I mean, the delivery guy comes in the afternoon to deliver something and he looks over to my sous-chef and asks for his signature on the check. Am I just some dumb-ass holding a coat?

JW: My mail is always addressed to Mr. Jody Williams.

AL: That happens to me all the time. I get my mail addressed to Anito Lo—not an a but an o: Mr. Anito Lo. And customers ask me, "Can you tell us about the chef's background? Is he from…"

Do women and men cook differently?

SJ: I think women cook different food, and I think women cook better food. It's more from the heart and more from the soul. I look at this whole molecular-gastronomy thing, and I'm like, "Boys with toys." They're just fascinated with technology and chemistry sets. I think we make better-tasting food. I'm sorry, I know that's politically incorrect.

RC: I have to agree. Women's food is, for the most part, more accessible, it's easier to understand, it's friendlier, it's more comforting, and it doesn't get bogged down in all these nutty freaking trends.

SJ: I find there's a lot of technique in male food.

AB: I have a friend from England who's a cook, and he said the food that's most moved him has always been cooked by a woman. Maybe because it's comfort food or it's very nurturing.

JW: Or maybe he just liked the idea of a woman cooking for him.

Anthony Bourdain's "Who Cooks?" and New York Magazine's "A Woman's Place?" both deal with gender imbalances in the kitchens of many top restaurants. Using the internet and resources available through your library, try to pinpoint the percentage of women who work in restaurant kitchens in the United States and the jobs that they hold. Does this data support the positions presented in "Who Cooks?" and "A Woman's Place?"

In "Who Cooks?" Bourdain argues that "line cooking is more about consistency, about mindless, unvarying repetition, the same series of tasks performed over and over and over again in exactly the same way." While Bourdain implicitly champions those who can pull off such disciplined cooking, these are the same reasons that many women have found cooking oppressive. From your experience and your readings, is the ability to perform mindlessly repetitive tasks generally valued? Do you think this characteristic is enviable? In what types of situations might this attribute be helpful? When might it be harmful?

Based on your reading of "Who Cooks?" and "A Woman's Place?"—and on any other pieces in this book that deal with food and gender—compose a brief essay in response to the following question: Why do you think that in the home, the kitchen and cooking are most commonly considered to be feminine, while in restaurants—especially high-end establishments—they are far more frequently hyper-masculine?

"Who Cooks?" and "A Woman's Place?" address gender issues in restaurant kitchens. But gender-based customer-service practices persist in the front of some restaurants, as well. Working with a group of classmates, conduct a gender-focused interview with a manager of a casual or fine-dining restaurant. Does the establishment encourage or require wait staff to serve women first? Why or why not? Are servers encouraged or discouraged to treat male and female customers differently? If so, how? Why? Does the manager notice if the restaurant serves more women or men? If so, to what does he/she attribute this? Does the manager detect behavioral differences between men and women as customers? If so, what are they? As a group, be prepared to report your findings to the rest of your class.

Marge Piercy has written seventeen volumes of poetry, seventeen novels, and a critically acclaimed memoir, Sleeping with Cats. According to her website, she has been a prominent player in many of "the major progressive political battles of our time, including the anti-Vietnam war and the women's movements," as well as protests against the war in Iraq. From her 1982 collection Circles on the Water: Selected Poems of Marge Piercy, "What's That Smell in the Kitchen?" points to the gendered expectations that still loom over the home kitchen.

WHAT'S THAT SMELL IN THE KITCHEN?

BY MARGE PIERCY

All over America women are burning dinners.
It's lambchops in Peoria; it's haddock
in Providence; it's steak in Chicago
tofu delight in Big Sur; red
rice and beans in Dallas.
All over America women are burning
food they're supposed to bring with calico
smile on platters glittering like wax.
Anger sputters in her brainpan, confined
but spewing out missiles of hot fat.
Carbonized despair presses like a clinker
from a barbecue against the back of her eyes.
If she wants to grill anything, it's
her husband spitted over a slow fire.
If she wants to serve him anything
it's a dead rat with a bomb in its belly
ticking like the heart of an insomniac.
Her life is cooked and digested,
nothing but leftovers in Tupperware.
Look, she says, once I was roast duck
on your platter with parsley but now I am Spam.
Burning dinner is not incompetence but war.

Piercy's poem stands out in this book in genre and style. After studying "What's That Smell in the Kitchen?" amplify Piercy's argument and rewrite the poem as an essay. Try to remain true to Piercy's theme as you make this transformation.

Food scholar and activist Michael Pollan has described Julia Child as an advocate for women's liberation through a particular style of cooking; however, according to Pollan, food marketers, have worked hard to create "the rhetoric of kitchen oppression." After reading Piercy's poem, watch with your group Sarah Haskins's take on women and cooking. (Here's a link to the Haskins video—*http://current.com/shows/infomania/89113716_ sarah-haskins-in-target-women-feeding-your-f-ing-family.htm*—or you can Google the search terms *sarah haskins target women feeding*). How does "the rhetoric of kitchen oppression" play out in Piercy's poem and Haskins' video? How does each author view the relationship between women and food? How does each make her argument? Do you find these texts persuasive? Why or why not?

Alice Waters, owner and founder of Chez Panisse Restaurant and Foundation in Berkeley, California, has championed local, organic food for more than thirty-eight years. She is introducing her ideas into public schools through Edible Education, a model garden and kitchen program. This essay was first published in the September 21, 2009, edition of The Nation.

A HEALTHY CONSTITUTION

By Alice Waters

I was moved by the way Morgan Spurlock framed a narrow long-distance shot down the corridor of a Beckley, West Virginia, middle school in his outstanding 2004 film, *Super Size Me*. The film is about the toll that fast and processed food takes on all of us. Clearly visible in the background of this particular shot were dozens of students, many of whom were overweight.

Perhaps it should come as no surprise that Beckley's cafeteria offers only processed food, which is high in fat, sodium and sugar and of very little nutritional value.

Contrast this with the Central Alternative High School in Appleton, Wisconsin. The school serves troubled youth, but teachers, parents and administrators found a way to turn things around; and when they did, discipline problems dropped sharply. Their secret? Instead of the usual processed meals, the school cafeteria offers fresh, locally grown, low-fat, low-sugar alternatives. The healthier meals are delicious. The students love them. They perform better in class and don't get sick as often.

We are learning that when schools serve healthier meals, they solve serious educational and health-related problems. But what's missing from the national conversation about school lunch reform is the opportunity to use food to teach values that are central to democracy. Better food isn't just about test scores, health and discipline. It is about preparing students for the responsibilities of citizenship.

Photo courtesy of chezparnisse.com

Alice Waters
Executive Chef, Founder and Owner of Chez Panisse

That's why we need to talk about edible education, not just school lunch reform. Edible education is a radical yet common-sense approach to teaching that integrates classroom instruction, school lunch, cooking and gardening into the studies of math, science, history and reading.

Edible education involves not only teaching children about where food comes from and how it is produced but giving them responsibilities in the school garden and kitchen. Students literally enjoy the fruits of their labor when the food they grow is served in healthy, delicious lunches that they can help prepare.

I learned this firsthand through the Chez Panisse Foundation—the organization I helped create to inspire a network of food activists around the world with edible education programs in their own communities. Here in Berkeley, I see children in our edible education program learn about responsibility, sharing and stewardship and become more connected to themselves and their peers. In the process, they come to embody the most important values of citizenship.

Listen to what one student named Charlotte has to say: "Next we went from the blue corn to the sweet corn and each picked an ear to grill. I must say it tasted really good, even without butter." Or Mati: "I think cleaning up is as important as eating. Cleaning up is sort of fun. And we can't just leave it for the teachers, because we made the mess." Or Jose: "I remember the first time I came to the kitchen. I was afraid to do anything. But then I realized, this is my kitchen. So then I started to enjoy it."

Charlotte, Mati and Jose are learning about so much more than lunch. They're learning that farmers depend on the land; we depend on farmers; and our nation depends on all of us. That cooperation with one another is necessary to nurture the community. And that, by setting the table for one another, we also take care of ourselves. School should be the place where we build democracy, not just by teaching about the Constitution but by becoming connected to our communities and the land in more meaningful ways.

In 1785, Thomas Jefferson declared that "Cultivators of the earth are the most valuable citizens. They are the most vigorous, the most independent, the most virtuous, and they are tied to their country and wedded to its liberty and interests by the most lasting bonds."

I believe he was right. The school cafeteria, kitchen and garden, like the town square, can and should be the place where we plant and nourish the values that guide our democracy. We need to join a delicious revolution that can reconnect our children to the table and to what it means to be a steward. This is the picture of a caring society, and this is the promise of edible education.

Use the internet or other sources to research whether there are any schools in your home state serving what Waters would call "fresh, locally grown, low-fat, low-sugar" meals. Are any schools in your state involved in anything like the "edible education" program she describes? Write a paragraph or two in which you summarize your findings.

Explain the link that Waters makes between healthy meals and learning. What kind of evidence does she offer to support these links? Do you think more evidence would have strengthened her argument?

FOOD

Eliot Coleman "has more than 40 years' experience in all aspects of organic farming," according to his website biography. The author of The New Organic Grower, Four Season Harvest, *and* The Winter Harvest Handbook, *Coleman, with Barbara Damrosch, operates a commercial year-round market garden, in addition to horticultural research projects, at Four Season Farm in Harborside, Maine. "Beyond Organic" was first published in the December/January 2002 issue of the sustainable lifestyle magazine* Mother Earth News.

BEYOND ORGANIC

BY ELIOT COLEMAN

New ideas, especially those that directly challenge an established orthodoxy, follow a familiar path. First, the orthodoxy says the new idea is rubbish. Then the orthodoxy attempts to minimize the new idea's increasing appeal. Finally, when the new idea proves unstoppable, the orthodoxy tries to claim the idea as its own. This is precisely the path organic food production has followed.

First, organic pioneers were ridiculed. Then, as evidence of the benefits of organic farming became more obvious to more people, mainstream chemical agriculture actively condemned organic ideas as not feasible. Now that the food-buying public has become enthusiastic about organically grown foods, the food industry wants to take over. Toward that end the U.S. Department of Agriculture-controlled national definition of "organic" is tailored to meet the marketing needs of organizations that have no connection to the agricultural integrity organic once represented. We now need to ask whether we want to be content with an "organic" food option that places the marketing concerns of corporate America ahead of nutrition, flavor and social benefits to consumers.

Author Eliot Coleman shows off greens and carrots grown at his farm.

When I started as an organic grower 35 years ago, organic was a way of thinking rather than a "profit center."

The decision to farm organically was a statement of faith in the wisdom of the natural world, to the quality of the crops and livestock, and to the nutritional benefits of properly cultivated food. It was obvious that good farming and exceptional food

only resulted from the care and nurturing practiced by the good farmer.

The initial development of organic farming during the first half of the 20th century arose from the gut feelings of farmers who were trying to reconcile the biological truths they saw in their own fields with the chemical dogma the agricultural science-of-the-moment was teaching. The farmers came to very different conclusions from those of the academic agronomists. The farmers worked on developing agricultural practices that harmonized with the direction in which their "unscientific" conclusions were leading them. Their goals were to grow the most nutritious food possible, while protecting the soil for future generations.

The development and refinement of those biologically based agricultural practices continues today. It's what makes this farming adventure so compelling. Each year I hope to do things better than I did last year because I will know Nature's systems better. But my delight in the intricacies of the natural world—my adventure into an ever deeper appreciation of the soil-plant-animal nutrition cycle and how to optimize it—is not acceptable to the homogenized mentality of mass marketing. The food giants that are taking over "organic" want a simplistic list of ingredients so they can do organic-by-the-numbers. They are derisive about what they label "belief systems," and they are loath to acknowledge that more farmer commitment is involved in producing real food than any number of approved inputs can encompass.

The transition of "organic" from small farm to big time is now upon us. Although getting toxic chemicals out of agriculture is an improvement we can all applaud, it only removes the negatives. The positive focus, enhancing the biological quality of the food produced, is nowhere to be seen. The new standards are based on what not to do rather than what to do. They will be administered through the USDA, whose director said recently, "Organic food does not mean it is superior, safer or more healthy than conventional food." Well, I still agree with the old-time organic pioneers. I believe that properly grown food is superior, safer and healthier. I also believe national certification bureaucracies are only necessary when food is grown by strangers in far away places rather than by neighbors you know. I further believe good, fresh food, grown locally by committed growers, is the very best to be found.

In my opinion, "organic" is now dead as a meaningful synonym for the highest quality food. Responsible growers need to identify not only that our food is grown to higher, more considered standards, but also that it is much fresher because it is grown right where it is sold. Therefore, we have come up with a new term, one we define to mean locally grown and unprocessed, in addition to exceptional quality. (See below.) It's a term we hope will be used, as "organic" was used when we began, by those local growers who accept that if you care first about the quality of what you produce, a market will always be there. We now sell our produce as "Authentic Food." We invite other serious growers to join us.

AUTHENTIC FOOD—BEYOND ORGANIC
A seal of quality from a farm near you

The label "organic" has lost the fluidity it used to hold for the growers more concerned with quality than the bottom line, and consumers more concerned with nutrition than a static set of standards for labeling. "Authentic" is meant to be the flexible term "organic" once was. It identifies fresh foods produced by local growers who want to focus on what they are doing, instead of what they aren't doing. (The word authentic derives from the Greek *authentes*: one who does things for him or herself.) The standards for a term like this shouldn't be set in stone, but here is what I would like for growers to focus on:

- All foods are produced by the growers who sell them.
- Fresh fruits and vegetables, milk, eggs and meat products are produced within a 50-mile radius of their place of their final sale.
- The seed and storage crops (grains, beans, nuts, potatoes, etc.) are produced within a 300-mile radius of their final sale.
- Only traditional processed foods such as cheese, wine, bread and lacto-fermented products may claim, "Made with authentic ingredients."
- The growers' fields, barns and greenhouses are open for inspection at any time, so customers, themselves, can be the certifiers of their food.

- All agricultural practices used on farms selling under the "authentic" label are chosen to produce foods of the highest nutritional quality.

- Soils are nourished, as in the natural world, with farm-derived organic matter and mineral particles from ground rock.

- Green manures and cover crops are included within broadly based crop rotations to maintain biological diversity.

- A "plant positive" rather than "pest negative" philosophy is followed, focusing on correcting the cause of problems rather than treating symptoms.

- Livestock are raised outdoors on grass-based pasture systems to the fullest extent possible.

- The goal is vigorous, healthy crops and livestock endowed with their inherent powers of vitality and resistance.

"Authentic" growers are committed to supplying food that is fresh, ripe, clean, safe and nourishing. "Authentic" farms are genetically modified organism-free zones. I encourage all small growers who believe in exceptional food and use local markets to use the word "authentic" to mean "beyond organic."

With a definition that stresses local, seller-grown and fresh, there is little likelihood that large-scale marketers can appropriate this concept.

-Eliot Coleman

Explore

When you see food labeled as organic, how do you assume it was produced? Research the USDA's definition of organic. Does it differ from your assumptions? If so, how? How does it differ from Coleman's definition?

Compose

Instead of organic—a term co-opted, he claims, by food marketers—Coleman creates a new label: Authentic Food—Beyond Organic. Design a visual argument that encapsulates these ideals and write a brief justification of your image. Look to the USDA's certified organic label as a starting place. In particular, think about how your design can call attention to the shortcomings of organic certification and emphasize the authenticity of fresh, locally-grown food.

Renee Brooks Catacalos and Kristi Bahrenburg Janzen co-published, from 2005-2009, Edible Chesapeake, a magazine devoted to the local food movement. They shared their experiment with eating local in the August/September 2006 edition of Mother Earth News.

SUBURBAN FORAGING: TWO FAMILIES EAT ONLY LOCAL

By Renee Brooks Catacalos and Kristi Bahrenburg Janzen

Amid increasing media buzz about the virtues of local food, we set out to discover how feasible it is to eat only local food all the time. As two suburban moms, we wanted to know if "eat local" was just a hollow marketing slogan or a real alternative for families who hope to enjoy the best seasonal foods, invest in the local economy and help the environment. How much would it cost? Would the kids go for it? Would our guests appreciate it?

Pledging to forage locally for a month, we defined "local" as grown and produced within a 150-mile radius of our homes in a Maryland suburb of Washington, D.C. We knew there were agricultural riches in our region. Yet much of what we discovered—or failed to discover—surprised us.

ENJOYING LOCAL PRODUCE

Our own small gardens, and those of friends and family, were our start. They yielded zesty nasturtium blossoms for salads, hot chile peppers, edamame, sweet cucumbers, herbs and other special produce. Renee's father had enough collards in his backyard to supply her all year. But, to feed our families of four, we needed a lot more.

We quickly became regulars at four producer-only farmers markets near our homes, where we picked up traditional favorites like corn on the cob, carrots bursting with flavor, mesclun greens, and various melons and berries. Kristi, eight months pregnant with her third child at the time, enjoyed the added convenience of weekly home delivery from two community supported agriculture farms (CSAs).

By shopping at the farmers markets, we began to make new observations about our food. The taste of local tree fruits was particularly striking. While they are typically grown using some pesticides due to the humid mid-Atlantic climate, the flavor was far superior to any shipped from across the country, organic or not. Kristi couldn't stop craving local award-winning peaches and cream. The kids reveled in the fruit too, tasting new varieties like metheny and cardinal plums. Renee's husband, Damon, especially enjoyed the long run of fresh apricots.

ROUNDING UP MEAT, FISH AND DAIRY

We also tapped directly into the farming community. Kristi ordered Amish organic meat, dairy, produce and other items like maple syrup through a buying club with a biweekly delivery 30 minutes from home. Renee was in the habit of taking her family on bimonthly field trips to Springfield Farm in Sparks, Maryland, a one-stop shop of sorts, selling grass-fed beef and lamb, pastured pork, chicken, and rabbits, and fresh free-range eggs.

Sometimes, we turned to various co-ops and health food stores, although no single shop carried all the local goods we wanted. Between them, however, we found many dairy products—both cows' and goats', both certified organic and conventional—from dairies in Maryland and Pennsylvania. They also carried some local eggs, fruits, vegetables, honey, maple syrup, and a little meat. We were pleased to find that our local conventional grocery stores offered some locally grown produce as well.

The Chesapeake Bay region is well-known for its seafood, but we didn't eat much of it during our experiment. Iconic products like blue crab and rockfish were simply too scarce and expensive. Renee had the occasional treat of a fresh croaker or two, a less famous but delicious regional fish, caught by her uncle, an avid sport-fisher. Through her CSA, Kristi received some wild-caught Alaskan salmon, hardly local, but environmentally friendly.

FACING AN INVOLUNTARY NO-CARBS DIET

The major challenges arose when we tried to find sources for pantry staples like flour, rice, corn meal, oats, barley, cereal, lentils, dried beans, nuts and dried fruit, as well as pasta and bread. Kristi did not eat wheat while pregnant, and was hoping to find spelt or rye.

Wheat required a three-hour round trip for a rendezvous with Western Maryland farmer Rick Hood who sold Renee a whole 10 pounds of wheat for just $2.50. We were stunned to find no commercial mills in Maryland grinding the millions of bushels of wheat and corn grown annually in the state. "The milling facilities in Maryland have died," Hood said.

With the help of a small kitchen grinder, Renee experienced the pleasure of baking with freshly ground wheat, although it required a lot of cleaning before grinding. She was relieved to eventually find Wade's Mill in Raphine, Virginia, via the internet. Millers Jim and Georgie Young stone-grind Virginia hard and soft wheat and happily fill mail orders with their old-fashioned twine-tied bags of flour. The only way to get local cornmeal was to drive to the tiny town of Westminster near the Pennsylvania border, where volunteers grind local corn at the historic water-powered Union Mills grist mill and sell it for $3 a bag.

Kristi was able to locate certified organic whole spelt, and whole rye flour grown without pesticides, both from Small Valley Milling in Halifax, Pennsylvania. The spelt was also ground and hulled locally. "I probably have the only dehulling facility in Pennsylvania," said farmer and mill owner Joel Steigman, who knows farmers who send their spelt to Michigan for dehulling.

We were, however, unable to find any bakers using local grains. When Kristi asked one bakery representative where their grains came from, he replied with a baffled, "Is that a trick question?" As a result, Kristi supplemented with breads that were at least locally baked and Renee stuck to her homemade bread.

Maryland's Eastern Shore yielded pecans from 100-year old trees at the Nuts to You farm, available every week at our local farmers market, as well as hybrid chestnuts from Delmarvelous Chestnuts, available by mail. Ground into flour, chestnuts pack a nutritional wallop and contribute to savory dishes like nutty-tasting crepes. Ordering nine jars of Virginia peanut butter online from The Peanut Shop of Williamsburg was probably the easiest purchase of the whole month.

As for legumes, we got them fresh all summer—edamame, crowder and black-eyed peas, baby lima and fava beans. Shelling the peas made the more finicky kids willing to at least give them a try. But we were told by more than one person in the know that the mid-Atlantic climate is not favorable for producing dried beans. And we were unable to find anybody offering the "grain, bean and seed" CSAs that we hear are available in some parts of the country.

TRADE-OFFS

We never felt deprived by cutting out tropical fruits, frozen convenience foods or typical snacks. The kids whined about their loss of cereal and pasta the first week, but as time went by, they got into the experiment (Laura Ingalls Wilder analogies helped!). They loved the open-pollinated Amish popcorn, and homemade potato and sweet potato chips. To satisfy their craving for sweets, Renee made peanut butter cookies using maple sugar, while Kristi baked cookies with whole spelt flour and pecans.

We did spend more time than usual in food preparation, including some experimental baking. Renee made "graham nuts" cereal using a recipe off the internet in response to her five-year-old's plea for cereal during the last week. Kristi's week-long experiment making sourdough rye only yielded two edible loaves, but piqued her interest in preparing the dark rye of her northern German ancestors.

Baking required us to make an exception to the 150-mile rule for leavening agents. We also granted ourselves additional exceptions, such as for oil and vinegar, salt and pepper, and tea. Kristi's husband, Bernd, couldn't do without coffee. Forgoing treats like refined sugar, chocolate and spices was difficult. But we earned a profound new appreciation for globally-traded flavor enhancers!

WILD PRICE RANGES AND HIDDEN COSTS

Price comparisons revealed that no one store was cheaper across the board. Price ranges of local foods were startlingly wide, and defied stereotypes. Whole Foods—known in some quarters as "Whole Paycheck"—actually yielded some relative bargains, while the smaller health food stores, food co-ops and farmers markets offered both bargains and sticker shocks.

To keep from busting our budgets, we watched for sales, and limited the high-end gourmet stuff, such as artisanal cheese. By being a neighborhood CSA coordinator, Kristi received her share of vegetables for free. We also made bulk purchases and grabbed seconds. Nob Hill Orchards, of Gerrardstown, West Virginia, for example, sells bulk berries at a discount, albeit frozen. Overripe peaches bought at half price from Harris Orchard, of Lothian, MD, made a fabulous crumble, and a half bushel of apple seconds for a mere $6 made quarts of fantastic applesauce.

Bulk discounts are especially valuable in purchasing meat. At Springfield Farm, rib eye steaks are $18 a pound and ground beef is $4 a pound, but Renee bought a 20-pound box of mixed roasts, steaks and ground meat for $3.95 a pound. Whole steers, sides or split quarters are as low as $2.50 a pound. "It really is a very good buy for people if they have the freezer space," said Valerie Lafferty, who runs the farm with her parents, David and Lilly Smith.

We intended to conserve fossil fuels by limiting the distance our food traveled to reach our tables. However, because the distribution system for local food is neither extensive nor coordinated, we did make lots of extra trips to pick up items from various suppliers. This was somewhat at odds with our intent, and we had to take the cost of gas into consideration.

At times, even though we paid a higher price for local food, we considered it a bargain. This was in part because the quality and flavor were so much better. But we also felt it worth paying more to help preserve small family farms and support locals who minimize environmental damage.

PUTTING IT ALL TOGETHER

Eating locally allowed us to see the unique culinary possibilities of our region, and taught us to stay creative and flexible in the kitchen. Sometimes, the vendor we were counting on didn't show up. Sometimes, supplies just ran out, or the weather brought crops to a premature end. Early on we learned not to get frustrated, but let available foods lead the way.

In the process, we came to love the simple pleasures of seeing the kids eat three plums for a snack instead of cheese curls and making toasted cheese sandwiches with local cheddar on homemade bread. We also relished bringing gourmet meals to the table from our local bounty.

Kristi's French beef stew using Amish meat, her own herbs, local red wine and bacon from Cibola Farms was the star of a dinner that included cabbage and tomato salad, and spaghetti squash sautéed in butter, garlic and onions. Family visiting from Montana enjoyed local breakfasts including French toast made with goats' milk and butter, and spelt pancakes.

One of the favorites at Renee's house was her sausage ragout, made with sweet Italian or rosemary-garlic-lamb sausage, fresh tomatoes, sweet corn right off the cob, and whatever fresh pea or bean was in season. Real old-fashioned buttermilk became, and remains, a staple in her house for pancakes, scones and cornbread.

At our end-of-experiment feast, everyone gobbled up award-winning goat cheeses from FireFly Farms, of Bittinger, Maryland, while sampling a variety of local wines, and beer from Franklin's, a microbrewery just down the road from our homes. Dragon tongue beans, red peppers, shitake mushrooms, herbs and pastured chicken thrown in a big pot produced a great stew. Blue potatoes, on discount at a local co-op, slathered in garlic and roasted, were a big hit with the kids.

Now that our one-month test is over, we've gone back to a few non-local items, like bananas and store-bought pasta. But we've retained a lot of our new habits, too. Once you get used to farm-fresh food, regular store-bought fare tastes remarkably bland. We're aiming to get more freezer space and planning to preserve more. We are really excited about the delicious fresh grain and bread-baking prospects too.

Perhaps even more gratifying, we've sparked conversations with local farmers and retailers about expanding the availability of local foods, and introducing new products, such as bread baked with local flour. As we've turned many of our friends, relatives and neighbors onto local food, we hope to see it become less of an adventure in foraging and more of an accessible choice for everyday eating.

EPILOGUE

Nearly a year after our all-or-nothing experiment, both our families still rely heavily on our local foodshed. We don't deny ourselves the pleasure of tropical fruits or fair trade coffee, but we buy local first and definitely purchase more local items than we used to.

The more we discuss local food, the more suppliers we discover. A conversation with the general manager of a neighborhood natural foods co-op, for example, resulted in higher-profile labeling of local products in the store. The bright yellow star that signifies "locally made" has led us to amazing discoveries, like tofu made from organic Virginia soybeans.

We've also found the general interest in local food to be widespread and growing. As many friends and neighbors continued to ask about our experiment, we recently hosted a neighborhood information session to share our months of research on local food. Thrilled to see more than 40 people attend, we quickly ran out of the 6 quarts of pick-your-own organic blueberries we offered as a snack, along with Virginia peanut butter and homemade wild yeast sourdough bread. Folks were not only interested in our food sources, but also wanted to hear how our children and husbands reacted to the local food, what our motivation was, and how we made it convenient and affordable.

We truly believe the more consumers seek local food, the more farmers will find it a viable economic opportunity, strengthening our local food system, local businesses and communities all at the same time.

Explore

Brooks Catacalos and Bahrenburg Janzen define "local" as within a 150-mile radius of their homes. How do your local farmers' markets define eating local? Try to find at least three markets in different regions and research their interpretations of "local." Are they different? If so, why do you think this is?

Collaborate

As a class, take the eat local challenge for a week and keep a daily blog of your experiences. Plan your eating strategy early and consult with fellow students about shopping, sales, bulk discounts, recipes, cooking, and sharing meals. How does your experiment compare to the authors'? What do you eat? What are your success and failure meals? Can you tell a discernible difference in terms of taste and quality of your food? In costs? Are you surprised at the offerings available to you locally? Can you tell a difference in your energy level? Do you have any non-local eating slip ups? Does eating local effect other aspects of your life? Are there ways in which local food producers could help you eat local on a permanent basis?

FOOD

Molly J. Dahm and Amy R. Shows are on the faculty of the Department of Family and Consumer Sciences at Lamar University in Beaumont, Texas. Aurelia V. Samonte works with Buckner Children and Family Services in Beaumont. They wrote this article for the Journal of American College Health *in 2009.*

ORGANIC FOODS: DO ECO-FRIENDLY ATTITUDES PREDICT ECO-FRIENDLY BEHAVIORS?

By Molly J. Dahm, Aurelia V. Samonte, and Amy R. Shows

CONSUMPTION OF ORGANIC FOODS

New research and mounting public interest have increased global awareness of organic food products. The primary consumers of organic food are women aged 30 to 45 who have children in the household and who are environmentally conscious.[1,2] However, interest in organic foods along with a sense of responsibility for the environment is growing among younger people, specifically college students, who are likely to identify issues that will influence their attitudes and activities in the future. Purchase and consumption of organic foods is another positive socially conscious behavior.[3]

One way universities in the United States have responded to students' increased interest in the environment is by adding organic foods to their menus. In fact, the presence of organic foods may ultimately factor into a student's choice of school.[4] Purchase and consumption of organic foods is one way students can practice eco-friendly behaviors. Eco-friendly behaviors might also be referred to as environmentally conscious behaviors, or "green consumption," e.g., legitimate means of exhibiting environmentally safe and responsible behaviors.[1] Other eco-friendly practices include recycling, energy conservation, water conservation, driving hybrid cars or carpooling, and ozone protection.

In this study, we examined the awareness (knowledge), attitudes, and behaviors of university students towards organic foods. We also attempted to determine if positive attitudes about organic foods and other environmental issues would predict consumption of organic foods and other healthy and eco-friendly practices.

FEDERAL STANDARDS FOR ORGANIC FOODS

The United States Department of Agriculture (USDA) informs consumers that the terms natural and organic are not interchangeable.[5] "Natural" refers to products without artificial flavorings, colorings, or chemical preservatives and minimal processing.[5] The USDA defines "organic foods" as products grown without the use of pesticides, synthetic fertilizers, sewage sludge, genetically modified organisms, or ionizing radiation.[5] The agency also requires that organic meat, poultry, eggs, and dairy products be produced from animals free of antibiotics or growth hormones.[6] The term "organic" is increasingly recognized as a trusted symbol of eco-friendly products.[7] Companies that handle or process organic foods for public consumption must be certified by the USDA.[5] The USDA Organic Seal (Figure 1) exhibits evidence of this certification.

FIGURE 1. USDA Organic Seal

Consumers who want to buy organic products should be able to correctly identify them. The USDA's label standards for organic products include 100% Organic (made with 100% organic ingredients); the word organic or the organic seal (95% organic); made with organic ingredients (minimum of 70% organic ingredients); and organic ingredients listed on the side panel (less than 70% organic ingredients).[5,6]

Other certification programs, such as Oregon's eco-labeling program and the system of integrated management (SIM) in Greece, promote eco-friendly products to consumers.[7] Loureiro et al.[8] studied consumers' level of awareness of certified products using eco-labeled apples and found that although general level of awareness about organic products was high (86%), awareness of the label meaning was limited.

CONSUMER ATTITUDES AND BEHAVIORS

Much of the current research about consumer attitudes and behaviors regarding organic foods has been conducted outside the United States, where scholars have noted consumer trust in organic products. In a Swedish study, attitudes towards and purchase of organic foods were strongly related to the perceived human health benefits of those foods.[2] Researchers in the United Kingdom found the term "organic" had emotional resonance for consumers in terms of personal well-being, health, benefits to the environment, and a healthy diet.[9,10]

As attitudes towards organic products evolve, values play an important but mixed role in how organic products are perceived.[11,12] Dreezens et al.[12] indicated that organic foods were viewed positively and associated with the values of welfare for all people and protection of nature. By contrast, Chryssohoidis and Krystallis[11] found that external values such as belonging to society were less important to consumers who purchased organic foods than internal values such as self-respect and enjoyment of life.

Consumer perception of appearance, taste, and texture of organic foods varies. In Northern Ireland, a focus group found organic products bland and lacking in color, yet stated that some organic foods, especially mixed vegetables, had desirable texture and flavor.[13] Researchers in the United Kingdom and Australia concluded that the taste of organic food was better than conventionally grown products[10] and that organic food had sensual qualities.[1]

As consumers develop more positive attitudes towards organic food, they are faced with purchase decisions. Studies have examined decision-making factors. Padel and Foster[9] concluded that the process is complex, and that motives and barriers may vary with product categories. Researchers have found a widespread perception of organic foods as expensive[10] and that the primary barrier to purchasing organic food was the consumer's level of personal disposable income.[14] Lockie et al.[1] suggested that increased education and household income is positively associated with the likelihood that an individual has consumed organic foods. However, other scholars have found that the main factor that hinders the purchase of organic food is limited availability of such foods.[11,15]

Consumer purchases of organic foods have increased. In 1994, Tregear et al.[18] found that 29% of the general public occasionally bought organic foods. A later study found that almost half of respondents purchased organic food on a regular basis.[13] Fruits and vegetables tend to be the first, and often the only, organic products that consumers buy.[9] Nonetheless, few consumers follow a diet that is mainly organic.[1]

OTHER ECO-FRIENDLY BEHAVIORS

There is some disagreement about whether there is an association between consumption of organic foods and other environmentally friendly behaviors. Davies et al.[14] found that consumers of organic foods were not necessarily concerned about the environment. However, two more recent studies found a significant relationship between environmentally friendly behaviors and organic food consumption.[1,2] In Oregon, the likelihood that a consumer will pay a premium for eco-labeled apples was positively associated with being environmentally conscious.[7] In Greece, willingness to pay for organic products was higher among consumers who placed importance on health.[8]

ATTITUDES AND BEHAVIORS OF YOUNG PEOPLE

In a study of 651 high school students in a major metropolitan area, Bissonnette and Contento[3] found that American adolescents had positive attitudes about organic foods. Students believed organic foods were healthier, tasted better, and were better for the environment. Yet their beliefs were not strong enough to urge them to act.[3]

Interest in organic foods or alternative food sources is evident in college age individuals who show an increasing enthusiasm for a healthy lifestyle and a sense of environmental responsibility.[4] Over the past 10 years, universities across the United States have introduced organic food options in response to student demand. For example, in 2000 the University of Wisconsin at Madison became the first major American public university to consistently place foods grown on local farms on the regular menu.[16]

In April 2006, the University of California-Berkeley received the nation's first organic certification on a college campus.[17] Menlo College uses nearly 100% organic foods and beverages on campus.[18] Also in 2006, Colorado State University and the University of Pennsylvania, in 2003, introduced student food venues that sell locally grown food. Oral Roberts University introduced its Green Cuisine brand in 2006, which includes organic salads, sandwiches, and packaged goods made from local food.[18,19] Thus, universities have responded to student demands for organic foods.

Because the literature is unclear whether consumer purchases follow upon knowledge and attitudes, the links between knowledge, attitudes, and behaviors with regard to organic foods (and other eco-friendly behaviors) should be explored to better understand and respond to consumer needs on college campuses.

METHOD

POPULATION AND SAMPLE

The population for this study was students at a mid-size university in the southeastern United States. The sample included 443 students who were enrolled in one of the mandated entry-level political science classes. Thus, the sampling method ensured a representative sample of the student body.

INSTRUMENTATION

The instrument, designed by the researchers, was 4 pages long and consisted of 28 items. Consent information was included on the first page of the instrument. Completion of the survey constituted consent to participate in the study. Study protocol was approved by the university's Institutional Review Board.

The first 5 questions requested demographic information: gender, race, age, student classification, place of residence, and income level. Four questions evaluated the subjects' awareness/knowledge of organic foods and 5 questions addressed the subjects' attitudes toward organic foods . In the fnal section, 12 questions sought information about student eating behaviors in relation to organic foods and healthy lifestyle practices, and 2 multipart questions examined attitudes and behaviors regarding other eco-friendly practices (recycling, energy conservation, water conservation, driving hybrid cars or carpooling).

PROCEDURES

After departmental approval was granted, researchers obtained permission from individual professors to administer the survey in each class. The average class size was 50 students. The survey was administered over a 2-week period to students present on the day of the survey. Several classes were not surveyed due to scheduling conflicts. A research assistant read procedures from a script before the surveys were distributed. Students were informed that the survey was voluntary and anonymous.

STATISTICAL ANALYSIS

Data analysis was conducted using SPSS Version 14.0 and Jump Version 5.0. Descriptive statistics described the sample and displayed frequencies of responses to survey items. Chi-square analysis was conducted to determine associations between categorical variables of interest. Linear regression tested whether student awareness/knowledge of organic foods predicted attitude about organic foods. Multiple correlation was used to examine the relationship between attitudes about organic foods and the purchase and consumption of those foods in different contexts. Linear regression and path analysis determined whether attitudes about organic foods might predict organic food purchase and consumption and healthy lifestyle practices. Finally, multiple correlation tested whether attitudes about other eco-friendly practices might predict corresponding behaviors.

RESULTS

The sample ($N = 443$) was 44.2% male and 55.8% female. The mean age of the group was 21.6 (SD ±5.01) years, with a range of 16 to 48 years. The racial/ethnic background of students was 54.6% White/Non-Hispanic, 30.6% African American, 7.0% Hispanic, 3.9% Asian, and 3.7% Other. The majority (59.5%) of the students were classified as sophomores. Approximately one third (27.4%) of the students lived on campus; the remaining students (72.6%) were commuters. Household annual income for 32.6% of the respondents was less than $20,000. Twenty-seven percent reported an annual household income of $20,001 to $50,000. The remainder (40.2%) reported annual income above $50,001.

When asked to identify the definition of the term "organic," 214 respondents (49.0%) selected the correct definition. Meanwhile, 138 (31.7%) recognized the USDA-approved organic seal. Knowledge of the correct definition of organic and recognition of the seal were significantly associated ($r_s = .161, p < .001$). Younger students (<21.6 years) were more likely to know the definition of organic and recognize the organic seal.

A majority of students knew that organic foods were available for purchase in grocery stores and in health food stores (72.2% and 79.0%, respectively). Few (9.7%) believed organic foods were available in restaurants. When asked in what form organic foods could be purchased (subjects could indicate all that applied), responses were as follows: produce (87.1%), grains (72.2%), dairy (53.5%), snacks (31.4%), meat (29.3%), beverages (28.2%), and candy (7.7%).

Most students (56.4%) were neutral in their opinion about organic foods, but 41.3% either "accept organic foods" or "only eat organic foods." Students ranked taste as the factor that influenced them most when selecting organic foods, followed by price, appearance, availability, and package information (Table 1). Approximately one third (31.1%) of respondents believed organic foods tasted the same as conventionally grown products, whereas 15.8% felt organic foods tasted better, and 12.3% felt organic foods tasted worse.

Only 20.7% of respondents reported they could purchase organic foods on campus, and few consumed more than 50% organic diets, no matter where they purchased foods. However, between 33.2% and 45.5% reported they purchased and consumed some organic foods on campus, in restaurants, or at home. The highest number (45.5%) purchased for consumption at home. When asked where they purchased organic foods 47.4% indicated the grocery store and 13.5% indicated a health food store. The frequencies of types of organic foods purchased were as follows: produce (40.4%), grains (28.2%), dairy (22.8%), drinks/beverages (20.8%), snacks (16.3%), and meat (13.8%). Interestingly, 50.5% of the students indicated they would support the use of organic foods on campus, and 64.0% reported they would buy organic foods if offered on campus.

TABLE 1. Frequency Rankings of Factors Affecting Purchase or Consumption of Organic Foods

Factors	Rankings	
	Frequency	Percentage (%)
Price	193	46.5
Taste	247	59.7
Appearance	120	29.0
Package Information	46	11.2
Other	12	5.6

There were significant positive relationships between knowledge of the definition of the term organic and opinion about organic foods (attitude) (r_s = .103, p < .05) and between recognition of the organic seal (knowledge) and opinion about organic foods (attitude) (r_s = .197, p < .01). Thus, awareness and attitude about organic foods were associated. Linear regression was used to test if the two knowledge variables predicted attitude. Results were significant (R^2 = .04, $F(2, 422)$ = 9.73, p < .000). Recognition of the seal was the strongest of the 2 predictors.

There was also a significant positive relationship between recognition of the organic seal and opinion about the taste of organic foods as compared to conventionally grown products (r_s = .298, p < .01). The relationship between the other knowledge variable (definition of organic) and attitude was not significant. Linear regression tested recognition of the organic seal as a predictor of attitude and was found to be significant (R^2 = .08, $F(2, 418)$ = 20.09, p < .000). When knowledge of the definition of organic was added as a predictor and tested in a second linear regression, model fit did not change significantly, corroborating the previous conclusion that the stronger predictor of attitude was recognition of the seal.

Multiple correlation was used to examine the relationship between attitudes about organic foods and subject responses about the support and purchase of organic foods (behavior) in different contexts (Table 2). Attitude towards organic foods was found to be significantly related to (1) purchase and consumption of organic foods on campus, (2) purchase and consumption of organic foods (usually in restaurants), and (3) purchase for consumption of foods at home.

Given the significant findings of the correlational analysis and linear regression, we conducted a path analysis (Figure 2) to determine whether attitudes toward organic foods would predict the three sets of purchase and consumption behaviors. Attitude was found to be a significant predictor (p < .01) of all 3 behaviors. Path analysis can be used to determine the significance and magnitude of the direct effect of predictor variables on response variables. It is an empirical tool to test cause-and-effect relationships.[20]

Attitude towards organic foods was found to be significantly related to student perceptions of whether or not they lead healthy lifestyles (r_s = .160, p < .01). A second path analysis was conducted to determine the direct effect of attitude towards organic foods on other healthy lifestyle practices. Significant path coefficients were calculated for relationships between positive attitudes towards organic foods and healthy diet ($p = .22$, $R^2 = 5.1\%$), regular exercise ($p = .14$, $R^2 = 2.1\%$), and consumption of organic foods ($p = .12$, $R^2 = 1.2\%$) only.

A final analysis examined the relationship between attitudes about other eco-friendly behaviors and the actual behaviors. Multiple correlation determined that most of the attitudes expressed about such behaviors were related to the practice of the behaviors. Further, in many instances, the respondents' attitudes about an eco-friendly behavior such as recycling and energy conservation were significantly related to supportive behaviors such as recycling, energy conservation, driving hybrid cars or carpooling, and ozone protection.

COMMENT

We found that students are relatively knowledgeable about organic food products and believe that organic foods are beneficial and necessary. Many expressed an interest in having more organic foods available on campus and indicated they would be willing to purchase organic foods if made available on campus. Contrary to the literature, we found that students were more likely to act upon the beliefs they expressed about both organic foods and eco-friendly behaviors.

Equal numbers of males and females knew the correct definition of the term organic, recognized the federal organic seal, and expressed a positive attitude towards organic foods. This finding varies somewhat from the literature, which identifies females as being more aware and having stronger attitudes about organic foods. Perhaps students, as a group, are simply more informed consumers. In future research, student responses could be compared to other types of consumers. When examining the relationship between awareness (knowledge) and attitude, we concluded that although many students selected the incorrect definition of the term organic, even these students had positive opinions in support of organic foods and other eco-friendly practices.

Most of the students in this study clustered in household income levels of under \$20,000 or above \$50,000. More than 30% of respondents from the upper household income levels reported that they "accept organic foods." Similar findings in the literature indicate higher levels of awareness and support for organic foods among individuals with higher incomes.[1] Future research should explore the degree to which parental/family household income affects student

TABLE 2. Correlation Between Attitude Towards and Consumption of Organic Food

	Attitude towards organic foods	Purchase and consumption of organic foods		
		On campus	Off campus (restaurant)	Home
Attitude towards organic foods	—	.284**	.309**	.298**
Purchase/consumption of organic foods				
On campus		—	.670**	.524**
Off campus (restaurant)			—	.641**
Home				—

Note. **p < .01.

consumer choices. More students under the mean age of 21.6 years knew the correct definition of the term organic and recognized the organic seal. Further, twice as many younger respondents expressed positive attitudes toward organic foods as those over the mean age. This suggests that younger people may seek out organic foods in various food environments or at least feel strongly about having them available. In that case, it makes sense that university food services should integrate more organic food options into their on-campus menus.

When subjects ranked factors that influenced their buying decisions, taste was reported to be most important, followed in order by price, appearance, availability, and package information. Consumers tend to associate health benefits with organic foods. Perhaps a younger, health-minded generation of educated consumers places more emphasis on quality (taste) and value (price). Such a conclusion might also support the fact that students knew of the availability of many forms of organic foods. A future study might include a tasting panel in which student consumers identify how various factors interact to influence the buying decision.

Students indicated that they purchased organic foods for consumption at home rather than on- or off-campus. This reinforces the finding that these foods were primarily purchased at grocery stores and health food stores. Produce, grains, and dairy products were the most often purchased organic foods. We agree with the literature that health educators need to work with food service operators to develop informational materials such as table tents and posters to help students learn about other organic food options.[9]

Few students followed an all-organic diet. Most purchased and consumed "50% or less" organic foods. However, more than half reported they would support the integration of organic foods into campus menus, and even more said they would buy organic foods if offered on campus. Such findings reinforce the current move on university campuses to provide more organic food options.

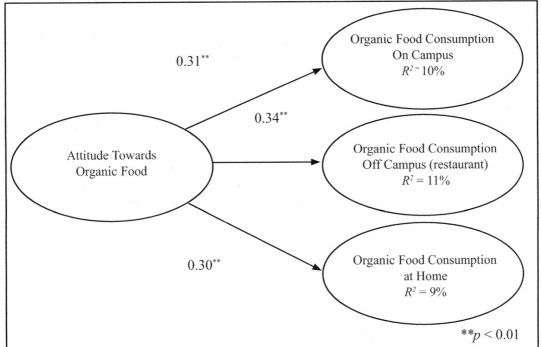

FIGURE 2. **Path analysis: Direct effect of student's overall attitude towards organic foods on their food choices on-campus, off-campus, and at home.**

Students who were able to identify the correct definition of the term organic and who recognized the USDA organic seal were more likely to have positive opinions supporting organic foods. Recognition of the organic seal was a significant predictor of the perception that organic foods tasted as good as or better than their conventionally grown counterparts. An extension of this study might involve a taste panel in which a perceptions and preferences are tested with respect to awareness and attitudes about organic foods.

The primary purpose of this study was to determine if student attitudes actually predicted corresponding behaviors with regard to organic foods. We concluded that they did. Tracking responses over time might determine if increased exposure to/availability of organic food products influences students who currently have no opinion about organic foods. We also found that students who had positive opinions about organic foods purchased and consumed such foods in different venues, most often for consumption at home. Therefore, attitude predicted behavior.

Botonaki et al.[7] suggested that consumers of organic foods are likely to engage in other healthy lifestyle practices. In our study, a positive attitude towards organic foods was significantly associated with consuming a healthy diet and exercising regularly. Health educators should further examine differences in student perceptions about healthy lifestyle practices.

Lockie et al.[1] and Magnusson et al.[2] found the consumption of organic foods and other environmentally conscious behaviors to be significantly related. In the present study, when students were asked about eco-friendly practices, there was a significant relationship between a positive attitude about these practices and the corresponding behavior. Clearly, students in this study not only felt strongly about environmental issues, but they also felt compelled towards eco-friendly practices.

CONCLUSION

In a classroom administration format or as with any self-report instrument, there is always the concern that subjects respond truthfully to the instrument items. In addition, the population characteristics of this university may be different. Thus, our findings that attitudes generally predicted behaviors must be interpreted with caution. Future studies should focus on other types of universities and track student behaviors to determine through observation whether a significant link with attitudes actually exists.

Some instrument items were forced choice, with an option to write in additional information. Forced-choice items do not accommodate the full range of possible responses even with the write-in option. For example, students with food allergies or concerns about chemical preservatives might opt for an organic diet. We may not have identified all opinions and factors relevant to the purchase and consumption of organic foods, healthy lifestyle or eco-friendly practices.

This study sampled students (young adults) from an American university, which helps to fill certain gaps in the literature. Additional research in the United

States about the attitudes towards purchase and consumption of organic foods is needed.

A principle finding in this study was that students are knowledgeable about organic foods and that they support the integration of organic foods into their menu choices and diets. Although less than half of the students indicated they purchased and consumed organic products in various environments, more than half of study respondents reported they would support the use of organic products on campus and would actually purchase organic foods on campus.

This sentiment is an important indicator for college and universities. There is already a demand for healthy food options on university campuses.[4,18] It seems that campus food services should evaluate not only their menu offerings, but even what they term healthy choices, in terms of organic food standards. It would be interesting to sample a portion of the respondents in this study in a year or so to determine if their attitudes have changed with regard to organic food purchase or consumption.

Our study focused on students as primary consumers; however, campuses also accommodate faculty and staff, many of whom may have opinions similar to those expressed by the students in this study. A future study might examine not only the opinions of other students on other campuses as well as other groups on campuses.

This study found that students who felt positively about organic foods were also inclined to behave accordingly. In other words, they were more likely to act on their opinions and choose to purchase and consume organic foods. Such a finding has implications for market food producers in general, in that college students are both consumers today as well as primary consumers of the future. It will be important to address this growing demand in more venues than college campuses.

REFERENCES

1. Lockie S, Lyons K, Lawrence G, Grice J. "Choosing organics: a path analysis of factors underlying the selection of organic food among Australian consumers." *Appetite.* 2004;43:135-146.

2. Magnusson M, Arvola A, Hursti U, Aberg L, Sjoden P. "Choice of organic foods is related to perceived consequences for human health and to environmentally friendly behaviour." *Appetite.* 2003;40:109-117.

3. Bissonnette M, Contento I. "Adolescents' perspectives and food choice behaviors in terms of the environmental impacts of food production practices: application of a psychosocial model." *J Nutr Educ.* 2001;33:72-82.

4. Horovitz B. "More university students call for organic, 'sustainable' food." *USAToday.com,* September 26, 2006:A.

5. "The National Organic Program." *Organic Food Standards and labels: The Facts.* Agricultural Marketing Service at United States Department of Agriculture Web site. http://www.ams.usda.gov/nop/Consumers/brochure.html. Accessed March 8, 2007.

6. "Organic faq." Organic.org Web site. http://www.organic.org/home/faq. Accessed October 17, 2006.

7. Botonaki A, Polymeros K, Tsakindou E, Mattas K. "The role of food quality certification on consumers' food choices." *Br Food J.* 2006;108:77-91.

8. Loureiro M, McCluskey J, Mittelhammer R. "Will consumers pay a premium for eco-labeled apples?" *J Consumer Affairs.* 2002;36:203-219.

9. Padel S, Foster C. "Exploring the gap between attitudes and behaviour: understanding why consumers buy or do not buy organic food." *Br Food J.* 2005;107:606-625.

10. Tregear A, Dent J, McGregor M. "The demand for organically-grown produce." *Br Food J.* 1994;96:21-26.

11. Chryssohoidis G, Krystallis, A. "Organic consumers' personal values research: testing and validating the list of values (LOV) scale and implementing a value-based segmentation task." *Food Qual Prefer.* 2005;16:585-599.

12. Dreezens E, Martijn C, Tenbult P, Kok G, de Vries N. "Food and values: an examination of values underlying attitudes toward genetically modified—and organically grown food products." *Appetite.* 2005;44:115-122.

13. Connor R, Douglas L. "Consumer attitudes to organic foods." *Nutr Food Sci.* 2001;31:254-258.

14. Davies A, Titterington A, Cochrane C. "Who buys organic food? A profile of the purchasers of organic food in Northern Ireland." *Br Food J.* 1995;97:17-24.

15. Fotopoulos, G. "Factors affecting the decision to purchase organic food." *J Eur-Marketing.* 2000;9:45-66.

16. "University of Wisconsin goes organic." *Organic Consumer Association Web site. 2006.* http://www.orgaanicconsumers.org/organic/uofw101903.cfm. Accessed October 17, 2006.

17. *Organic certification.* University of California-Berkeley Web site. http://caldining. berkeley.edu/environment.organic.cert.html. Accessed October 17, 2006.

18. Horovitz B. "Organic food spreads across campuses." *USAToday*, September 27, 2006:B2.

19. Oral Roberts Fall 2007 "Student Catalogue." *Oral Roberts University* Web site. http://www.oru.edu/catalog/ORU.hb0203.pdf. Accessed March 12, 2008.

20. Williams W, Jones M, Demment M. "A concise table for path analysis statistics." *Agron J.* 1990;82:1022-1024.

Research your college or university's organic food offerings. What are they? Were you aware of these offerings (or lack thereof) before your research? If organic options are available, do you regularly take advantage of them? Next, find other schools that stock local or organic food for students. What different levels of commitment to organic food in higher education do you find in your research?

Evaluate Dahm, Samonte, and Shows's findings. Do you consider their primary and secondary research convincing? How does the evidence they provide differ from previous essays you've read? How do the stylistic conventions of an academic journal article influence your reading experience? What are the methodological strengths and weakness of the piece? Did you find the survey questions appropriate? Were there any questions that you think should have been added? Were the charts useful in explaining the researchers' results? Given the scope that they identify, do you think this is a significant study? Do you find this type of article more or less convincing than, for instance, a personal narrative like "Suburban Foraging" (on page 117)? Why?

Robert Paarlberg is B.F. Johnson professor of political science at Wellesley College, an associate at Harvard University's Weatherhead Center for International Affairs, and author of Food Politics: What Everyone Needs to Know. *He wrote this essay for the May/June 2010 edition of* Foreign Policy *magazine.*

ATTENTION WHOLE FOODS SHOPPERS

BY ROBERT PAARLBERG

From Whole Foods recyclable cloth bags to Michelle Obama's organic White House garden, modern eco-foodies are full of good intentions. We want to save the planet. Help local farmers. Fight climate change—and childhood obesity, too. But though it's certainly a good thing to be thinking about global welfare while chopping our certified organic onions, the hope that we can help others by changing our shopping and eating habits is being wildly oversold to Western consumers. Food has become an elite preoccupation in the West, ironically, just as the most effective ways to address hunger in poor countries have fallen out of fashion.

Helping the world's poor feed themselves is no longer the rallying cry it once was. Food may be today's cause célèbre, but in the pampered West, that means trendy causes like making food "sustainable"—in other words, organic, local, and slow.

Appealing as that might sound, it is the wrong recipe for helping those who need it the most. Even our understanding of the global food problem is wrong these days, driven too much by the single issue of international prices. In April 2008, when the cost of rice for export had tripled in just six months and wheat reached its highest price in 28 years, a *New York Times* editorial branded this a "World Food Crisis." World Bank President Robert Zoellick warned that high food prices would be particularly damaging in poor countries, where "there is no margin for survival." Now that international rice prices are down 40 percent from their peak and wheat prices have fallen by more than half, we too quickly conclude that the crisis is over. Yet 850 million people in poor countries were chronically undernourished before the 2008 price spike, and the number is even larger now, thanks in part to last year's global recession. This is the real food crisis we face.

It turns out that food prices on the world market tell us very little about global hunger. International markets for food, like most other international markets, are used most heavily by the well-to-do, who are far from hungry. The majority of truly undernourished people—62 percent, according to the U.N. Food and Agriculture Organization—live in either Africa or South Asia, and most are small farmers or rural landless laborers living in the countryside of Africa and South Asia. They are significantly shielded from global price fluctuations both by the trade policies of their own governments and by poor roads and infrastructure. In Africa, more than 70 percent of rural households are cut off from the closest urban markets because, for instance, they live more than a 30-minute walk from the nearest all-weather road.

Poverty—caused by the low income productivity of farmers' labor—is the primary source of hunger in Africa, and the problem is only getting worse. The number of "food insecure" people in Africa (those consuming less than 2,100 calories a day) will increase 30 percent over the next decade without significant reforms, to 645 million, the U.S. Agriculture Department projects.

What's so tragic about this is that we know from experience how to fix the problem. Wherever the rural poor have gained access to improved roads, modern seeds, less expensive fertilizer, electrical power, and better schools and clinics, their productivity and their income have increased. But recent efforts to deliver such essentials have been undercut by deeply misguided (if sometimes well-meaning) advocacy against agricultural modernization and foreign aid.

In Europe and the United States, a new line of thinking has emerged in elite circles that opposes bringing improved seeds and fertilizers to traditional farmers and opposes linking those farmers more closely to international markets. Influential food writers, advocates, and celebrity restaurant owners are repeating the mantra that "sustainable food" in the future must be organic, local, and slow. But guess what: rural Africa already has such a system, and it doesn't work. Few smallholder farmers in Africa use any synthetic chemicals, so their food is *de facto* organic. High transportation costs force them to purchase and sell almost all of their food locally. And food preparation is painfully slow. The result is nothing to celebrate: average income levels of only $1 a day and a one-in-three chance of being malnourished.

If we are going to get serious about solving global hunger, we need to de-romanticize our view of pre-industrial food and farming. And that means learning to appreciate the modern, science-intensive, and highly capitalized agricultural system we've developed in the West. Without it, our food would be more expensive and less safe. In other words, a lot like the hunger-plagued rest of the world.

ORIGINAL SINS

Thirty years ago, had someone asserted in a prominent journal or newspaper that the Green Revolution was a failure, he or she would have been quickly dismissed. Today the charge is surprisingly common. Celebrity author and eco-activist Vandana Shiva claims the Green Revolution has brought nothing to India except "indebted and discontented farmers." A 2002 meeting in Rome of 500 prominent international NGOs, including Friends of the Earth and Greenpeace, even blamed the Green Revolution for the rise in world hunger. Let's set the record straight.

The development and introduction of high-yielding wheat and rice seeds into poor countries, led by American scientist Norman Borlaug and others in the 1960s and '70s, paid huge dividends. In Asia these new seeds lifted tens of millions of small farmers out of desperate poverty and finally ended the threat of periodic famine. India, for instance, doubled its wheat production between 1964 and 1970 and was able to terminate all dependence on international food aid by 1975. As for indebted and discontented farmers, India's rural poverty rate fell from 60 percent to just 27 percent today. Dismissing these great achievements as a "myth" (the official view of Food First, a California-based organization that campaigns globally against agricultural modernization) is just silly.

It's true that the story of the Green Revolution is not everywhere a happy one. When powerful new farming technologies are introduced into deeply unjust rural social systems, the poor tend to lose out. In Latin America, where access to good agricultural land and credit has been narrowly controlled by traditional elites, the improved seeds made available by the Green Revolution increased income gaps. Absentee landlords in Central America, who previously allowed peasants to plant subsistence crops on underutilized land, pushed them off to sell or rent the land to commercial growers who could turn a profit using the new seeds. Many of the displaced rural poor became slum dwellers. Yet even in Latin America, the prevalence of hunger declined more than 50 percent between 1980 and 2005.

In Asia, the Green Revolution seeds performed just as well on small non-mechanized farms as on larger farms. Wherever small farmers had sufficient access to credit, they took up the new technology just as quickly as big farmers, which led to dramatic income gains and no increase in inequality or social friction. Even poor landless laborers gained, because more abundant crops meant more work at harvest time, increasing rural wages. In Asia, the Green Revolution was good for both agriculture and social justice.

And Africa? Africa has a relatively equitable and secure distribution of land, making it more like Asia than Latin America and increasing the chances that improvements in farm technology will help the poor. If Africa were to put greater resources into farm technology, irrigation, and rural roads, small farmers would benefit.

ORGANIC MYTHS

There are other common objections to doing what is necessary to solve the real hunger crisis. Most revolve around caveats that purist critics raise regarding food systems in the United States and Western Europe. Yet such concerns, though well-intentioned, are often misinformed and counterproductive—especially when applied to the developing world.

Take industrial food systems, the current bugaboo of American food writers. Yes, they have many unappealing aspects, but without them food would be not only less abundant but also less safe. Traditional food systems lacking in reliable refrigeration and sanitary packaging are dangerous vectors for diseases. Surveys over the past several decades by the Centers for Disease Control and Prevention have found that the U.S. food supply became steadily safer over time, thanks in part to the introduction of industrial-scale technical improvements. Since 2000, the incidence of E. coli contamination in beef has fallen 45 percent. Today in the United States, most hospitalizations and fatalities from unsafe food come not from sales of contaminated products at supermarkets, but from the mishandling or improper preparation of food inside the home. Illness outbreaks from contaminated foods sold in stores still occur, but the fatalities are typically quite limited. A nationwide scare over unsafe spinach in 2006 triggered the virtual suspension of all fresh and bagged spinach sales, but only three known deaths were recorded. Incidents such as these command attention in part because they are now so rare. Food Inc. should be criticized for filling our plates with too many foods that are unhealthy, but not foods that are unsafe.

Where industrial-scale food technologies have not yet reached into the developing world, contaminated food remains a major risk. In Africa, where many foods are still purchased in open-air markets (often uninspected, unpackaged, unlabeled, unrefrigerated, unpasteurized, and unwashed), an estimated 700,000 people die every year from food- and water-borne diseases, compared with an estimated 5,000 in the United States.

Food grown organically—that is, without any synthetic nitrogen fertilizers or pesticides—is not an answer to the health and safety issues. *The American Journal of Clinical Nutrition* last year published a study of 162 scientific papers from the past 50 years on the health benefits of organically grown foods and found no nutritional advantage over conventionally grown foods. According to the Mayo Clinic, "No conclusive evidence shows that organic food is more nutritious than is conventionally grown food."

Health professionals also reject the claim that organic food is safer to eat due to lower pesticide residues. Food and Drug Administration surveys have revealed that the highest dietary exposures to pesticide residues on foods in the United States are so trivial (less than one one-thousandth of a level that would cause toxicity) that the safety gains from buying organic are insignificant. Pesticide exposures remain a serious problem in the developing world, where farm chemical use is not as well regulated, yet even there they are more an occupational risk for unprotected farmworkers than a residue risk for food consumers.

When it comes to protecting the environment, assessments of organic farming become more complex. Excess nitrogen fertilizer use on conventional farms in the United States has polluted rivers and created a "dead zone" in the Gulf of Mexico, but halting synthetic nitrogen fertilizer use entirely (as farmers must do in the United States to get organic certification from the Agriculture Department) would cause environmental problems far worse.

Here's why: Less than 1 percent of American cropland is under certified organic production. If the other 99 percent were to switch to organic and had to fertilize crops without any synthetic nitrogen fertilizer, that would require a lot more composted animal manure. To supply enough organic fertilizer, the U.S. cattle population would have to increase roughly fivefold. And because those animals would have to be raised organically on forage crops, much of the land in the lower 48 states would need to be converted to pasture. Organic field crops also have lower yields per hectare. If Europe tried to feed itself organically, it would need an additional 28 million hectares of cropland, equal to all of the remaining forest cover in France, Germany, Britain, and Denmark combined.

Mass deforestation probably isn't what organic advocates intend. The smart way to protect against nitrogen runoff is to reduce synthetic fertilizer applications with taxes, regulations, and cuts in farm subsidies, but not try to go all the way to zero as required by the official organic standard. Scaling up registered organic farming would be on balance harmful, not helpful, to the natural environment.

Not only is organic farming less friendly to the environment than assumed, but modern conventional farming is becoming significantly more sustainable. High-tech farming in rich countries today is far safer for the environment, per bushel of production, than it was in the 1960s, when Rachel Carson criticized the indiscriminate farm use of DDT in her environmental classic, *Silent Spring*. Thanks in part to Carson's devastating critique, that era's most damaging insecticides were banned and replaced by chemicals that could be applied in lower volume and were less persistent in the environment. Chemical use in American agriculture peaked soon thereafter, in 1973. This was a major victory for environmental advocacy.

And it was just the beginning of what has continued as a significant greening of modern farming in the United States. Soil erosion on farms dropped sharply in the 1970s with the introduction of "no-till" seed planting, an innovation that also reduced dependence on diesel fuel because fields no longer had to be plowed every spring. Farmers then began conserving water by moving to drip irrigation and by leveling their fields with lasers to minimize wasteful runoff. In the 1990s, GPS equipment was added to tractors, autosteering the machines in straighter paths and telling farmers exactly where they were in the field to within one square meter, allowing precise adjustments in chemical use. Infrared sensors were brought in to detect the greenness of the crop, telling a farmer exactly how much more (or less) nitrogen might be needed as the growing season went forward. To reduce wasteful nitrogen use, equipment was developed that can insert fertilizers into the ground at exactly the depth needed and in perfect rows, only where it will be taken up by the plant roots.

These "precision farming" techniques have significantly reduced the environmental footprint of modern agriculture relative to the quantity of food being produced. In 2008, the Organization for Economic Cooperation and Development published a review of the "environmental performance of agriculture" in the world's 30 most advanced industrial countries—those with the most highly capitalized and science-intensive farming systems. The results showed that between 1990 and 2004, food production in these countries continued to increase (by 5 percent in volume), yet adverse environmental impacts were reduced in every category. The land area taken up by farming declined 4 percent, soil erosion from both wind and water fell, gross greenhouse gas emissions from farming declined 3 percent, and excessive nitrogen fertilizer use fell 17 percent. Biodiversity also improved, as increased numbers of crop varieties and livestock breeds came into use.

SEEDING THE FUTURE

Africa faces a food crisis, but it's not because the continent's population is growing faster than its potential to produce food, as vintage Malthusians such as environmental advocate Lester Brown and advocacy organizations such as Population Action International would have it. Food production in Africa is vastly less than the region's known potential, and that is why so many millions are going hungry there. African farmers still use almost no fertilizer; only 4 percent of cropland has been improved with irrigation; and most of the continent's cropped area is not planted with seeds improved through scientific plant breeding, so cereal yields are only a fraction of what they could be. Africa is failing to keep up with population growth not because it has exhausted its potential, but instead because too little has been invested in reaching that potential.

One reason for this failure has been sharply diminished assistance from international donors. When agricultural modernization went out of fashion among elites in the developed world beginning in the 1980s, development assistance to farming in poor countries collapsed. Per capita food production in Africa was declining during the 1980s and 1990s and the number of hungry people on the continent was doubling, but the U.S. response was to withdraw development assistance and simply ship more food aid to Africa. Food aid doesn't help farmers become more productive—and it can create long-term dependency. But in recent years, the dollar value of U.S. food aid to Africa has reached 20 times the dollar value of agricultural development assistance.

The alternative is right in front of us. Foreign assistance to support agricultural improvements has a strong record of success, when undertaken with purpose. In the 1960s, international assistance from the Rockefeller Foundation, the Ford Foundation, and donor governments led by the United States made Asia's original Green Revolution possible. U.S. assistance to India provided critical help in improving agricultural education, launching a successful agricultural extension service, and funding advanced degrees for Indian agricultural specialists at universities in the United States. The U.S. Agency for International Development, with the World Bank, helped finance fertilizer plants and infrastructure projects, including rural roads and irrigation. India could not have done this on its own—the country was on the brink of famine at the time and dangerously dependent on food aid. But instead of suffering a famine in 1975, as some naysayers had predicted, India that year celebrated a final and permanent end to its need for food aid.

Foreign assistance to farming has been a high-payoff investment everywhere, including Africa. The World Bank has documented average rates of return on investments in agricultural research in Africa of 35 percent a year, accompanied by significant reductions in poverty. Some research investments in African agriculture have brought rates of return estimated at 68 percent. Blind to these realities, the United States cut its assistance to agricultural research in Africa 77 percent between 1980 and 2006.

When it comes to Africa's growing hunger, governments in rich countries face a stark choice: They can decide to support a steady new infusion of financial and technical assistance to help local governments and farmers become more productive, or they can take a "worry later" approach and be forced to address hunger problems with increasingly expensive shipments of food aid. Development skeptics and farm modernization critics keep pushing us toward this unappealing second path. It's time for leaders with vision and political courage to push back.

Explore

Locate images from the book *Hungry Planet: What the World Eats* (Some can be found at *www.time.com/time/photogallery/0,29307,1626519,00. html*, or you can do a Google search for the terms *hungry planet time*). Of these families pictured, who do you think eats local? Who eats organic? Which of the diets do you think is most nutritious? Which is the most environmentally sustainable? How do these images affect your reading of Paarlberg's essay?

Invent

Read "Declare Your Independence" by Joel Salatin (it starts on page 175). After considering the arguments Paarlberg and Salatin make, develop a list of points that each author might use to respond to the other's central claim.

Collaborate

In contrast to most of the readings in this collection, Paarlberg throws his support behind industrial food production: "If we are going to get serious about solving global hunger, we need to de-romanticize our view of pre-industrial food and farming ...Without it, our food would be more expensive and less safe." Centering on the issue of the best farming practices to address world hunger, divide your class between support for industrial farming techniques and support for organic practices. Research your positions and counterarguments and come together to debate the issue. Pay attention to the credibility of the sources you and your classmates use. After the debate, write a brief summary of the arguments made. Who had the best supported points? Were you persuaded by any of your opponents' arguments?

Matthew Scully served as special assistant and deputy director of speechwriting to President George W. Bush and also wrote for vice presidents Dick Cheney and Dan Quayle. The author of Dominion: The Power of Man, the Suffering of Animals, and the Call to Mercy, *Scully wrote this essay for the May 23, 2005, issue of* The American Conservative *magazine.*

FEAR FACTORIES: THE CASE FOR COMPASSIONATE CONSERVATISM—FOR ANIMALS

BY MATTHEW SCULLY

A few years ago I began a book about cruelty to animals and about factory farming in particular, problems that had been in the back of my mind for a long while. At the time I viewed factory farming as one of the lesser problems facing humanity—a small wrong on the grand scale of good and evil but too casually overlooked and too glibly excused.

This view changed as I acquainted myself with the details and saw a few typical farms up close. By the time I finished the book, I had come to view the abuses of industrial farming as a serious moral problem, a truly rotten business for good reason passed over in polite conversation. Little wrongs, when left unattended, can grow and spread to become grave wrongs, and precisely this had happened on our factory farms.

The result of these ruminations was *Dominion: The Power of Man, the Suffering of Animals, and the Call to Mercy.* And though my tome never quite hit the bestseller lists, there ought to be some special literary prize for a work highly recommended in both the *Wall Street Journal* and *Vegetarian Teen.* When you enjoy the accolades of PETA and *Policy Review,* Deepak Chopra and Gordon Liddy, Peter Singer and Charles Colson, you can at least take comfort in the diversity of your readership.

The book also provided an occasion for fellow conservatives to get beyond their dislike for particular animal-rights groups and to examine cruelty issues on the merits. Conservatives have a way of dismissing the subject, as if where animals are concerned nothing very serious could ever be at stake. And though it is not exactly true that liberals care more about these issues—you are no more likely to find reflections or exposés concerning cruelty in *The Nation* or *The New Republic* than in any journal of the Right—it is assumed that animal-protection causes are a project of the Left, and that the proper conservative position is to stand warily and firmly against them.

I had a hunch that the problem was largely one of presentation and that by applying their own principles to animal-welfare issues conservatives would find plenty of reasons to be appalled. More to the point, having acknowledged the problems of cruelty, we could then support reasonable remedies. Conservatives, after all, aren't shy about discoursing on moral standards or reluctant to translate the most basic of those standards into law. Setting aside the distracting rhetoric of animal rights, that's usually what these questions come down to: what moral standards should guide us in our treatment of animals, and when must those standards be applied in law?

Industrial livestock farming is among a whole range of animal-welfare concerns that extends from canned trophy-hunting to whaling to product testing on animals to all sorts of more obscure enterprises like the exotic-animal trade and the factory farming of bears in China for bile believed to hold medicinal and aphrodisiac powers. Surveying the various uses to which animals are put, some might be defensible, others abusive and unwarranted, and it's the job of any conservative who attends to the subject to figure out which are which. We don't need novel theories of rights to do this. The usual distinctions that conservatives draw between moderation and excess, freedom and license, moral goods and material goods, rightful power and the abuse of power, will all do just fine.

As it is, the subject hardly comes up at all among conservatives, and what commentary we do hear usually takes the form of ridicule directed at animal-rights groups. Often conservatives side instinctively with any animal-related industry and those involved, as if a thing is right just because someone can make money off it or as if our sympathies belong always with the men just because they are men.

I had an exchange once with an eminent conservative columnist on this subject. Conversation turned to my book and to factory farming. Holding his hands out in the "stop" gesture, he said, "I don't want to know." Granted, life on the factory farm is no one's favorite subject, but conservative writers often have to think about things that are disturbing or sad. In this case, we have an intellectually formidable fellow known to millions for his stern judgments on every matter of private morality and public policy. Yet nowhere in all his writings do I find any treatment of any cruelty issue, never mind that if you asked him he would surely agree that cruelty to animals is a cowardly and disgraceful sin.

And when the subject is cruelty to farmed animals—the moral standards being applied in a fundamental human enterprise—suddenly we're in forbidden territory and "I don't want to know" is the best he can do. But don't we have a responsibility to know? Maybe the whole subject could use his fine mind and his good heart.

As for the rights of animals, rights in general are best viewed in tangible terms, with a view to actual events and consequences. Take the case of a hunter in Texas named John Lockwood, who has just pioneered the online safari. At his canned-hunting ranch outside San Antonio, he's got a rifle attached to a camera and the camera wired up to the Internet, so that sportsmen going to *Live-shot.com* will actually be able to fire at baited animals by remote control from their computers. "If the customer were to wound the animal," explains the *San Antonio Express-News*, "a staff person on site could finish it off." The "trophy mounts" taken in these heroics will then be prepared and shipped to the client's door, and if it catches on Lockwood will be a rich man.

Very much like animal farming today, the hunting "industry" has seen a collapse in ethical standards, and only in such an atmosphere could Lockwood have found inspiration for this latest innovation—denying wild animals the last shred of respect. Under the laws of Texas and other states, Lockwood and others in his business use all sorts of methods once viewed as shameful: baits, blinds, fences to trap hunted animals in ranches that advertise a "100-percent-guaranteed kill." Affluent hunters like to unwind by shooting cage-reared pheasants, ducks, and other birds, firing away as the fowl of the air are released before them like skeet, with no limit on the day's kill. Hunting supply stores are filled with lures, infrared lights, high-tech scopes, and other gadgetry to make every man a marksman.

Lockwood doesn't hear anyone protesting those methods, except for a few of those nutty activist types. Why shouldn't he be able to offer paying customers this new hunting experience as well? It is like asking a smut-peddler to please have the decency to keep children out of it. Lockwood is just one step ahead of the rest, and there is no standard of honor left to stop him.

First impressions are usually correct in questions of cruelty to animals, and here most of us would agree that *Live-shot.com* does not show our fellow man at his best. We would say that the whole thing is a little tawdry and even depraved, that the creatures Lockwood has "in stock" are not just commodities. We would say that these animals deserve better than the fate he has in store for them.

As is invariably the case in animal-rights issues, what we're really looking for are safeguards against cruel and presumptuous people. We are trying to hold people to their obligations, people who could spare us the trouble if only they would recognize a few limits on their own conduct.

Conservatives like the sound of "obligation" here, and those who reviewed *Dominion* were relieved to find me arguing more from this angle than from any notion of rights. "What the PETA crowd doesn't understand," Jonah Goldberg wrote, "or what it deliberately confuses, is that human compassion toward animals is an obligation of humans, not an entitlement for animals." Another commentator put the point in religious terms: "[W]e have a moral duty to respect the animal world as God's handiwork, treating animals with 'the mercy of our Maker' … but mercy and respect for animals are completely different from rights for animals—and we should never confuse the two." Both writers confessed they were troubled by factory farming and concluded with the uplifting thought that we could all profit from further reflection on our obligation of kindness to farm animals.

The only problem with this insistence on obligation is that after a while it begins to sounds like a hedge against actually being held to that obligation. It leaves us with a high-minded attitude but no accountability, free to act on our obligations or to ignore them without consequences, personally opposed to cruelty but unwilling to impose that view on others.

Treating animals decently is like most obligations we face, somewhere between the most and the least important, a modest but essential requirement to living with integrity. And it's not a good sign when arguments are constantly turned to precisely how much is mandatory and how much, therefore, we can manage to avoid.

If one is using the word "obligation" seriously, moreover, then there is no practical difference between an obligation on our end not to mistreat animals and an entitlement on their end not to be mistreated by us. Either way, we are required to do and not do the same things. And either way, somewhere down the logical line, the entitlement would have to arise from a recognition of the inherent dignity of a living creature. The moral standing of our fellow creatures may be humble, but it is absolute and not something within our power to confer or withhold. All creatures sing their Creator's praises, as this truth is variously expressed in the Bible, and are dear to Him for their own sakes.

A certain moral relativism runs through the arguments of those hostile or indifferent to animal welfare—as if animals can be of value only for our sake, as utility or preference decrees. In practice, this outlook leaves each person to decide for himself when animals rate moral concern. It even allows us to accept or reject such knowable facts about animals as their cognitive and emotional capacities, their conscious experience of pain and happiness.

Elsewhere in contemporary debates, conservatives meet the foe of moral relativism by pointing out that, like it or not, we are all dealing with the same set of physiological realities and moral truths. We don't each get to decide the facts of science on a situational basis. We do not each go about bestowing moral value upon things as it pleases us at the moment. Of course, we do not decide moral truth at all: we discern it. Human beings in their moral progress learn to appraise things correctly, using reasoned moral judgment to perceive a prior order not of our devising.

C.S. Lewis in *The Abolition of Man* calls this "the doctrine of objective value, the belief that certain attitudes are really true, and others really false, to the kind of thing the universe is and the kind of things we are." Such words as honor, piety, esteem, and empathy do not merely describe subjective states of mind, Lewis reminds us, but speak to objective qualities in the world beyond that merit those attitudes in us. "[T]o call children delightful or old men venerable," he writes, "is not simply to record a psychological fact about our own parental or filial emotions at the moment, but to recognize a quality which demands a certain response from us whether we make it or not."

This applies to questions of cruelty as well. A kindly attitude toward animals is not a subjective sentiment; it is the correct moral response to the objective value of a fellow creature. Here, too, rational and virtuous conduct consists in giving things their due and in doing so consistently. If one animal's pain—say, that of one's pet—is real and deserving of sympathy, then the pain of essentially identical animals is also meaningful, no matter what conventional distinctions we have made to narrow the scope of our sympathy. If it is wrong to whip a dog or starve a horse or bait bears for sport or grossly abuse farm animals, it is wrong for all people in every place.

The problem with moral relativism is that it leads to capriciousness and the despotic use of power. And the critical distinction here is not between human obligations and animal rights, but rather between obligations of charity and obligations of justice.

Active kindness to animals falls into the former category. If you take in strays or help injured wildlife or donate to animal charities, those are fine things to do, but no one says you should be compelled to do them. Refraining from cruelty to animals is a different matter, an obligation of justice not for us each to weigh for ourselves. It is not simply unkind behavior, it is unjust behavior, and the prohibition against it is non-negotiable. Proverbs reminds us of this—"a righteous man regardeth the life of his beast, but the tender mercies of the wicked are cruel"—and the laws of America and of every other advanced nation now recognize the wrongfulness of such conduct with our cruelty statutes. Often applying felony-level penalties to protect certain domestic animals, these state and federal statutes declare that even though your animal may elsewhere in the law be defined as your property, there are certain things you may not do to that creature, and if you are found harming or neglecting the animal, you will answer for your conduct in a court of justice.

There are various reasons the state has an interest in forbidding cruelty, one of which is that cruelty is degrading to human beings. The problem is that many thinkers on this subject have strained to find indirect reasons to explain why cruelty is wrong and thereby to force animal cruelty into the category of the victimless crime. The most common of these explanations asks us to believe that acts of cruelty matter only because the cruel person does moral injury to himself or sullies his character—as if the man is our sole concern and the cruelly treated animal is entirely incidental.

Once again, the best test of theory is a real-life example. In 2002, Judge Alan Glenn of Tennessee's Court of Criminal Appeals heard the case of a married couple named Johnson, who had been found guilty of cruelty to 350 dogs lying sick, starving, or dead in their puppy-mill kennel—a scene videotaped by police. Here is Judge Glenn's response to their supplications for mercy:

The victims of this crime were animals that could not speak up to the unbelievable conduct of Judy Fay Johnson and Stanley Paul Johnson that they suffered. Several of the dogs have died and most had physical problems such as intestinal worms, mange, eye problems, dental problems and emotional problems and socialization problems ... . Watching this video of the conditions that these dogs were subjected to was one of the most deplorable things this Court has observed. ...

[T]his Court finds that probation would not serve the ends of justice, nor be in the best interest of the public, nor would this have a deterrent effect for such gross behavior. ... The victims were particularly vulnerable. You treated the victims with exceptional cruelty. ...

There are those who would argue that you should be confined in a house trailer with no ventilation or in a cell three-by-seven with eight or ten other inmates with no plumbing, no exercise and no opportunity to feel the sun or smell fresh air. However, the courts of this land have held that such treatment is cruel and inhuman, and it is. You will not be treated in the same way that you treated these helpless animals that you abused to make a dollar.

Only in abstract debates of moral or legal theory would anyone quarrel with Judge Glenn's description of the animals as "victims" or deny that they were entitled to be treated better. Whether we call this a "right" matters little, least of all to the dogs, since the only right that any animal could possibly exercise is the right to be free from human abuse, neglect, or, in a fine old term of law, other "malicious mischief." What matters most is that prohibitions against human cruelty be hard and binding. The sullied souls of the Johnsons are for the Johnsons to worry about. The business of justice is to punish their offense and to protect the creatures from human wrongdoing. And in the end, just as in other matters of morality and justice, the interests of man are served by doing the right thing for its own sake.

There is only one reason for condemning cruelty that doesn't beg the question of exactly why cruelty is a wrong, a vice, or bad for our character: that the act of cruelty is an intrinsic evil. Animals cruelly dealt with are not just things, not just an irrelevant detail in some self-centered moral drama of our own. They matter in their own right, as they matter to their Creator, and the wrongs of cruelty are wrongs done to them. As *The Catholic Encyclopedia* puts this point, there is a "direct and essential sinfulness of cruelty to the animal world, irrespective of the results of such conduct on the character of those who practice it."

Our cruelty statutes are a good and natural development in Western law, codifying the claims of animals against human wrongdoing, and, with the wisdom of men like Judge Glenn, asserting those claims on their behalf. Such statutes, however, address mostly random or wanton acts of cruelty. And the persistent animal-welfare questions of our day center on institutional cruelties—on the vast and systematic mistreatment of animals that most of us never see.

Having conceded the crucial point that some animals rate our moral concern and legal protection, informed conscience turns naturally to other animals—creatures entirely comparable in their awareness, feeling, and capacity for suffering. A dog is not the moral equal of a human being, but a dog is definitely the moral equal of a pig, and it's only human caprice and economic convenience that say otherwise. We have the problem that these essentially similar creatures are treated in dramatically different ways, unjustified even by the very different purposes we have assigned to them. Our pets are accorded certain protections from cruelty, while the nameless creatures in our factory farms are hardly treated like animals at all. The challenge is one of consistency, of treating moral equals equally, and living according to fair and rational standards of conduct.

Whatever terminology we settle on, after all the finer philosophical points have been hashed over, the aim of the exercise is to prohibit wrongdoing. All rights, in practice, are protections against human wrongdoing, and here too the point is to arrive at clear and consistent legal boundaries on the things that one may or may not do to animals, so that every man is not left to be the judge in his own case.

More than obligation, moderation, ordered liberty, or any of the other lofty ideals we hold, what should attune conservatives to all the problems of animal cruelty—and especially to the modern factory farm—is our worldly side. The great virtue of conservatism is that it begins with a realistic assessment of human motivations. We know man as he is, not only the rational creature but also, as Socrates told us, the rationalizing creature, with a knack for finding an angle, an excuse, and a euphemism. Whether it's the pornographer who thinks himself a free-speech champion or the abortionist who looks in the mirror and sees a reproductive health-care services provider, conservatives are familiar with the type.

So we should not be all that surprised when told that these very same capacities are often at work in the things that people do to animals—and all the more so in our $125 billion a year livestock industry. The human mind, especially when there is money to be had, can manufacture grand excuses for the exploitation of other human beings. How much easier it is for people to excuse the wrongs done to lowly animals.

Where animals are concerned, there is no practice or industry so low that someone, somewhere, cannot produce a high-sounding reason for it. The sorriest little miscreant who shoots an elephant, lying in wait by the water hole in some canned-hunting operation, is just "harvesting resources," doing his bit for "conservation." The swarms of government-subsidized Canadian seal hunters slaughtering tens of thousands of newborn pups—hacking to death these unoffending creatures, even in sight of their mothers—offer themselves as the brave and independent bearers of tradition. With the same sanctimony and deep dishonesty, factory-farm corporations like Smithfield Foods, ConAgra, and Tyson Foods still cling to countrified brand names for their labels—Clear Run Farms, Murphy Family Farms, Happy Valley—to convince us and no doubt themselves, too, that they are engaged in something essential, wholesome, and honorable.

Yet when corporate farmers need barbed wire around their Family Farms and Happy Valleys and laws to prohibit outsiders from taking photographs (as is the case in two states) and still other laws to exempt farm animals from the definition of "animals" as covered in federal and state cruelty statues, something is amiss. And if conservatives do nothing else about any other animal issue, we should attend at least to the factory farms, where the suffering is immense and we are all asked to be complicit.

If we are going to have our meats and other animal products, there are natural costs to obtaining them, defined by the duties of animal husbandry and of veterinary ethics. Factory farming came about when resourceful men figured out ways of getting around those natural costs, applying new technologies to raise animals in conditions that would otherwise kill them by deprivation and disease. With no laws to stop it, moral concern surrendered entirely to economic calculation, leaving no limit to the punishments that factory farmers could inflict to keep costs down and profits up. Corporate farmers hardly speak anymore of "raising" animals, with the modicum of personal care that word implies. Animals are "grown" now, like so many crops. Barns somewhere along the way became "intensive confinement facilities" and the inhabitants mere "production units."

The result is a world in which billions of birds, cows, pigs, and other creatures are locked away, enduring miseries they do not deserve, for our convenience and pleasure. We belittle the activists with their radical agenda, scarcely noticing the radical cruelty they seek to redress.

At the Smithfield mass-confinement hog farms I toured in North Carolina, the visitor is greeted by a bedlam of squealing, chain rattling, and horrible roaring. To maximize the use of space and minimize the need for care, the creatures are encased row after row, 400 to 500 pound mammals trapped without relief inside iron crates seven feet long and 22 inches wide. They chew maniacally on bars and chains, as foraging animals will do when denied straw, or engage in stereotypical nest-building with the straw that isn't there, or else just lie there like broken beings. The spirit of the place would be familiar to police who raided that Tennessee puppy-mill run by Stanley and Judy Johnson, only instead of 350 tortured animals, millions—and the law prohibits none of it.

Efforts to outlaw the gestation crate have been dismissed by various conservative critics as "silly," "comical," "ridiculous." It doesn't seem that way up close. The smallest scraps of human charity—a bit of maternal care, room to roam outdoors, straw to lie on—have long since been taken away as costly luxuries, and so the pigs know the feel only of concrete and metal. They lie covered in their own urine and excrement, with broken legs from trying to escape or just to turn, covered with festering sores, tumors, ulcers, lesions, or what my guide shrugged off as the routine "pus pockets."

C.S. Lewis's description of animal pain—"begun by Satan's malice and perpetrated by man's desertion of his post"—has literal truth in our factory farms because they basically run themselves through the wonders of automation, and the owners are off in spacious corporate offices reviewing their spreadsheets. Rarely are the creatures' afflictions examined by a vet or even noticed by the migrant laborers charged with their care, unless of course some ailment threatens production—meaning who cares about a lousy ulcer or broken leg, as long as we're still getting the piglets?

Kept alive in these conditions only by antibiotics, hormones, laxatives, and other additives mixed into their machine-fed swill, the sows leave their crates only to be driven or dragged into other crates, just as small, to bring forth their piglets. Then it's back to the gestation crate for another four months, and so on back and forth until after seven or eight pregnancies they finally expire from the punishment of it or else are culled with a club or bolt-gun.

As you can see at *www.factoryfarming.com/gallery.htm*, industrial livestock farming operates on an economy of scale, presupposing a steady attrition rate. The usual comforting rejoinder we hear—that it's in the interest of farmers to take good care of their animals—is false. Each day, in every confinement farm in America, you will find cull pens littered with dead or dying creatures discarded like trash.

For the piglets, it's a regimen of teeth cutting, tail docking (performed with pliers, to heighten the pain of tail chewing and so deter this natural response to mass confinement), and other mutilations. After five or six months trapped in one of the grim warehouses that now pass for barns, they're trucked off, 355,000 pigs every day in the life of America, for processing at a furious pace of thousands per hour by migrants who use earplugs to muffle the screams. All of these creatures, and billions more across the earth, go to their deaths knowing nothing of life, and nothing of man, except the foul, tortured existence of the factory farm, having never even been outdoors.

But not to worry, as a Smithfield Foods executive assured me, "They love it." It's all "for their own good." It is a voice conservatives should instantly recognize, as we do when it tells us that the fetus feels nothing. Everything about the picture shows bad faith, moral sloth, and endless excuse-making, all readily answered by conservative arguments.

We are told "they're just pigs" or cows or chickens or whatever and that only urbanites worry about such things, estranged as they are from the realities of rural life. Actually, all of factory farming proceeds by a massive denial of reality—the reality that pigs and other animals are not just production units to be endlessly exploited but living creatures with natures and needs. The very modesty of those needs—their humble desires for straw, soil, sunshine—is the gravest indictment of the men who deny them.

Conservatives are supposed to revere tradition. Factory farming has no traditions, no rules, no codes of honor, no little decencies to spare for a fellow creature. The whole thing is an abandonment of rural values and a betrayal of honorable animal husbandry—to say nothing of veterinary medicine, with its sworn oath to "protect animal health" and to "relieve animal suffering."

Likewise, we are told to look away and think about more serious things. Human beings simply have far bigger problems to worry about than the well being of farm animals, and surely all of this zeal would be better directed at causes of human welfare.

You wouldn't think that men who are unwilling to grant even a few extra inches in cage space, so that a pig can turn around, would be in any position to fault others for pettiness. Why are small acts of kindness beneath us, but not small acts of cruelty? The larger problem with this appeal to moral priority, however, is that we are dealing with suffering that occurs through human agency. Whether it's miserliness here, carelessness there, or greed throughout, the result is rank cruelty for which particular people must answer.

Since refraining from cruelty is an obligation of justice, moreover, there is no avoiding the implications. All the goods invoked in defense of factory farming, from the efficiency and higher profits of the system to the lower costs of the products, are false goods unjustly derived. No matter what right and praiseworthy things we are doing elsewhere in life, when we live off a cruel and disgraceful thing like factory farming, we are to that extent living unjustly, and that is hardly a trivial problem.

For the religious-minded, and Catholics in particular, no less an authority than Pope Benedict XVI has explained the spiritual stakes. Asked recently to weigh in on these very questions, Cardinal Ratzinger told German journalist Peter Seewald that animals must be respected as our "companions in creation." While it is licit to use them for food, "we cannot just do whatever we want with them. ... Certainly, a sort of industrial use of creatures, so that geese are fed in such a way as to produce as large a liver as possible, or hens live so packed together that they become just caricatures of birds, this degrading of living creatures to a commodity seems to me in fact to contradict the relationship of mutuality that comes across in the Bible."

Factory farmers also assure us that all of this is an inevitable stage of industrial efficiency. Leave aside the obvious reply that we could all do a lot of things in life more efficiently if we didn't have to trouble ourselves with ethical restraints. Leave aside, too, the tens of billions of dollars in annual federal subsidies that have helped megafarms undermine small family farms and the decent communities that once surrounded them and to give us the illusion of cheap products. And never mind the collateral damage to land, water, and air that factory farms cause and the more billions of dollars it costs taxpayers to clean up after them. Factory farming is a predatory enterprise, absorbing profit and externalizing costs, unnaturally propped up by political influence and government subsidies much as factory-farmed animals are unnaturally sustained by hormones and antibiotics.

Even if all the economic arguments were correct, conservatives usually aren't impressed by breathless talk of inevitable progress. I am asked sometimes how a conservative could possibly care about animal suffering in factory farms, but the question is premised on a liberal caricature of conservatism—the assumption that, for all of our fine talk about moral values, "compassionate conservatism" and the like, everything we really care about can be counted in dollars. In the case of factory farming, and the conservative's blithe tolerance of it, the caricature is too close to the truth.

Exactly how far are we all prepared to follow these industrial and technological advances before pausing to take stock of where things stand and where it is all tending? Very soon companies like Smithfield plan to have tens of millions of cloned animals in their factory farms. Other companies are at work genetically engineering chickens without feathers so that one day all poultry farmers might be spared the toil and cost of de-feathering their birds. For years, the many shills for our livestock industry employed in the "Animal Science" and "Meat Science" departments of rural universities (we used to call them Animal Husbandry departments) have been tampering with the genes of pigs and other

"No one who does not profit from them," writes Matthew Scully, "can look at our modern factory farms or frenzied slaughter plants or agricultural laboratories with their featherless chickens and fear-free pigs and think, 'Yes, this is humanity at our finest—exactly as things should be.'"

animals to locate and expunge that part of their genetic makeup that makes them stressed in factory farm conditions—taking away the desire to protect themselves and to live. Instead of redesigning the factory farm to suit the animals, they are redesigning the animals to suit the factory farm.

Are there no boundaries of nature and elementary ethics that the conservative should be the first to see? The hubris of such projects is beyond belief, only more because of the foolish and frivolous goods to be gained—blood-free meats and the perfect pork chop.

No one who does not profit from them can look at our modern factory farms or frenzied slaughter plants or agricultural laboratories with their featherless chickens and fear-free pigs and think, "Yes, this is humanity at our finest— exactly as things should be." Devils charged with designing a farm could hardly have made it more severe. Least of all should we look for sanction in Judeo-Christian morality, whose whole logic is one of gracious condescension, of the proud learning to be humble, the higher serving the lower, and the strong protecting the weak.

Those religious conservatives who, in every debate over animal welfare, rush to remind us that the animals themselves are secondary and man must come first are exactly right—only they don't follow their own thought to its moral conclusion. Somehow, in their pious notions of stewardship and dominion, we always seem to end up with singular moral dignity but no singular moral accountability to go with it.

Lofty talk about humanity's special status among creatures only invites such questions as: what would the Good Shepherd make of our factory farms? Where does the creature of conscience get off lording it over these poor creatures so mercilessly? "How is it possible," as Malcolm Muggeridge asked in the years when factory farming began to spread, "to look for God and sing his praises while insulting and degrading his creatures? If, as I had thought, all lambs are the Agnus Dei, then to deprive them of light and the field and their joyous frisking and the sky is the worst kind of blasphemy."

The writer B.R. Meyers remarked in *The Atlantic*, "research could prove that cows love Jesus, and the line at the McDonald's drive-through wouldn't be one sagging carload shorter the next day …. Has any generation in history ever been so ready to cause so much suffering for such a trivial advantage? We deaden our consciences to enjoy—for a few minutes a day—the taste of blood, the feel of our teeth meeting through muscle."

That is a cynical but serious indictment, and we must never let it be true of us in the choices we each make or urge upon others. If reason and morality are what set human beings apart from animals, then reason and morality must always guide us in how we treat them, or else it's all just caprice, unbridled appetite with the pretense of piety. When people say that they like their pork chops, veal, or foie gras just too much ever to give them up, reason hears in that the voice of gluttony, willfulness, or at best moral complaisance. What makes a human being human is precisely the ability to understand that the suffering of an animal is more important than the taste of a treat.

Of the many conservatives who reviewed *Dominion*, every last one conceded that factory farming is a wretched business and a betrayal of human responsibility. So it should be a short step to agreement that it also constitutes a serious issue of law and public policy. Having granted that certain practices are abusive, cruel, and wrong, we must be prepared actually to do something about them.

Among animal activists, of course, there are some who go too far—there are in the best of causes. But fairness requires that we judge a cause by its best advocates instead of making straw men of the worst. There isn't much money in championing the cause of animals, so we're dealing with some pretty altruistic people who on that account alone deserve the benefit of the doubt.

If we're looking for fitting targets for inquiry and scorn, for people with an angle and a truly pernicious influence, better to start with groups like Smithfield Foods (my candidate for the worst corporation in America in its ruthlessness to people and animals alike), the National Pork Producers Council (a reliable Republican contributor), or the various think tanks in Washington subsidized by animal-use industries for intellectual cover.

After the last election, the National Pork Producers Council rejoiced, "President Bush's victory ensures that the U.S. pork industry will be very well positioned for the next four years politically, and pork producers will benefit from the long-term results of a livestock agriculture-friendly agenda." But this is no tribute. And millions of good people who live in what's left of America's small family-farm communities would themselves rejoice if the president were to announce that he is prepared to sign a bipartisan bill making some basic reforms in livestock agriculture.

Bush's new agriculture secretary, former Nebraska Gov. Mike Johanns, has shown a sympathy for animal welfare. He and the president might both be surprised at the number and variety of supporters such reforms would find in the Congress, from Republicans like Chris Smith and Elton Gallegly in the House to John Ensign and Rick Santorum in the Senate, along with Democrats such as Robert Byrd, Barbara Boxer, or the North Carolina congressman who called me in to say that he, too, was disgusted and saddened by hog farming in his state.

If such matters were ever brought to President Bush's attention in a serious way, he would find in the details of factory farming many things abhorrent to the Christian heart and to his own kindly instincts. Even if he were to drop into relevant speeches a few of the prohibited words in modern industrial agriculture (cruel, humane, compassionate), instead of endlessly flattering corporate farmers for virtues they lack, that alone would help to set reforms in motion.

We need our conservative values voters to get behind a Humane Farming Act so that we can all quit averting our eyes. This reform, a set of explicit federal cruelty statutes with enforcement funding to back it up, would leave us with farms we could imagine without wincing, photograph without prosecution, and explain without excuses.

The law would uphold not only the elementary standards of animal husbandry but also of veterinary ethics, following no more complicated a principle than that pigs and cows should be able to walk and turn around, fowl to move about and spread their wings, and all creatures to know the feel of soil and grass and the warmth of the sun. No need for labels saying "free-range" or "humanely raised." They will all be raised that way. They all get to be treated like animals and not as unfeeling machines.

On a date certain, mass confinement, sow gestation crates, veal crates, battery cages, and all such innovations would be prohibited. This will end livestock agriculture's moral race to the bottom and turn the ingenuity of its scientists toward compassionate solutions. It will remove the federal support that unnaturally serves agribusiness at the expense of small farms. And it will shift economies of scale, turning the balance in favor of humane farmers—as those who run companies like Wal-Mart could do right now by taking their business away from factory farms.

In all cases, the law would apply to corporate farmers a few simple rules that better men would have been observing all along: we cannot just take from these creatures, we must give them something in return. We owe them a merciful death, and we owe them a merciful life. And when human beings cannot do something humanely, without degrading both the creatures and ourselves, then we should not do it at all.

Invent

Read through the essay and identify the sources that Scully uses to support his argument. Why do you think he chose these particular people and publications? How do these sources help him reach his intended audience?

Compose

Do you think of animal rights as a conservative position? How does Scully build and support his case that cruelty to animals, especially in the factory farming system, should be a conservative cause? Write a short essay in which you describe your expectations of an animal rights activist and how Scully's essay affected those expectations.

Collaborate

In his essay, Scully writes: "If reason and morality are what set human beings apart from animals, then reason and morality must always guide us in how we treat them, or else it's all just caprice, unbridled appetite with the pretense of piety." Working with a group, discuss what Scully means by this. Then, look online to find other conservative positions on animal rights. How do these differ from Scully's?

Nicolette Hahn Niman, a lawyer and livestock rancher, is the author of Righteous Porkchop: Finding a Life and Good Food Beyond Factory Farms. *She wrote this opinion column for* The New York Times *in October of 2009.*

THE CARNIVORE'S DILEMMA

BY NICOLETTE HAHN NIMAN

Bolinas, Calif.—Is eating a hamburger the global warming equivalent of driving a Hummer? This week an article in The Times of London carried a headline that blared: "Give Up Meat to Save the Planet." Former Vice President Al Gore, who has made climate change his signature issue, has even been assailed for omnivorous eating by animal rights activists.

It's true that food production is an important contributor to climate change. And the claim that meat (especially beef) is closely linked to global warming has received some credible backing, including by the United Nations and University of Chicago. Both institutions have issued reports that have been widely summarized as condemning meat-eating.

But that's an overly simplistic conclusion to draw from the research. To a rancher like me, who raises cattle, goats and turkeys the traditional way (on grass), the studies show only that the prevailing methods of producing meat— that is, crowding animals together in factory farms, storing their waste in giant lagoons and cutting down forests to grow crops to feed them—cause substantial greenhouse gases. It could be, in fact, that a conscientious meat eater may have a more environmentally friendly diet than your average vegetarian.

So what is the real story of meat's connection to global warming? Answering the question requires examining the individual greenhouse gases involved: carbon dioxide, methane and nitrous oxides.

Carbon dioxide makes up the majority of agriculture-related greenhouse emissions. In American farming, most carbon dioxide emissions come from fuel burned to operate vehicles and equipment. World agricultural carbon emissions, on the other hand, result primarily from the clearing of woods for crop growing and livestock grazing. During the 1990s, tropical deforestation in Brazil, India, Indonesia, Sudan and other developing countries caused 15 percent to 35 percent of annual global fossil fuel emissions.

Much Brazilian deforestation is connected to soybean cultivation. As much as 70 percent of areas newly cleared for agriculture in Mato Grosso State in Brazil is being used to grow soybeans. Over half of Brazil's soy harvest is controlled by a handful of international agribusiness companies, which ship it all over the world for animal feed and food products, causing emissions in the process.

Meat and dairy eaters need not be part of this. Many smaller, traditional farms and ranches in the United States have scant connection to carbon dioxide emissions because they keep their animals outdoors on pasture and make little use of machinery. Moreover, those farmers generally use less soy than industrial operations do, and those who do often grow their own, so there are no emissions from long-distance transport and zero chance their farms contributed to deforestation in the developing world.

In contrast to traditional farms, industrial livestock and poultry facilities keep animals in buildings with mechanized systems for feeding, lighting, sewage flushing, ventilation, heating and cooling, all of which generate emissions. These factory farms are also soy guzzlers and acquire much of their feed overseas. You can reduce your contribution to carbon dioxide emissions by avoiding industrially produced meat and dairy products.

Unfortunately for vegetarians who rely on it for protein, avoiding soy from deforested croplands may be more difficult: as the Organic Consumers Association notes, Brazilian soy is common (and unlabeled) in tofu and soymilk sold in American supermarkets.

Methane is agriculture's second-largest greenhouse gas. Wetland rice fields alone account for as much 29 percent of the world's human-generated methane. In animal farming, much of the methane comes from lagoons of liquefied manure at industrial facilities, which are as nauseating as they sound.

This isn't a problem at traditional farms. "Before the 1970s, methane emissions from manure were minimal because the majority of livestock farms in the U.S. were small operations where animals deposited manure in pastures and corrals," the Environmental Protection Agency says. The E.P.A. found that with the rapid rise of factory farms, liquefied manure systems became the norm and methane emissions skyrocketed. You can reduce your methane emissions by seeking out meat from animals raised outdoors on traditional farms.

Critics of meat-eating often point out that cattle are prime culprits in methane production. Fortunately, the cause of these methane emissions is understood, and their production can be reduced.

Much of the problem arises when livestock eat poor quality forages, throwing their digestive systems out of balance. Livestock nutrition experts have demonstrated that by making minor improvements in animal diets (like providing nutrient-laden salt licks) they can cut enteric methane by half. Other practices, like adding certain proteins to ruminant diets, can reduce methane production per unit of milk or meat by a factor of six, according to research at Australia's University of New England. Enteric methane emissions can also be substantially reduced when cattle are regularly rotated onto fresh pastures, researchers at University of Louisiana have confirmed.

Finally, livestock farming plays a role in nitrous oxide emissions, which make up around 5 percent of this country's total greenhouse gases. More than three-quarters of farming's nitrous oxide emissions result from manmade fertilizers. Thus, you can reduce nitrous oxide emissions by buying meat and dairy products from animals that were not fed fertilized crops—in other words, from animals raised on grass or raised organically.

In contrast to factory farming, well-managed, non-industrialized animal farming minimizes greenhouse gases and can even benefit the environment. For example, properly timed cattle grazing can increase vegetation by as much as 45 percent, North Dakota State University researchers have found. And grazing by large herbivores (including cattle) is essential for well-functioning prairie ecosystems, research at Kansas State University has determined.

Additionally, several recent studies show that pasture and grassland areas used for livestock reduce global warming by acting as carbon sinks. Converting croplands to pasture, which reduces erosion, effectively sequesters significant amounts of carbon. One analysis published in the journal Global Change Biology showed a 19 percent increase in soil carbon after land changed from cropland to pasture. What's more, animal grazing reduces the need for the fertilizers and fuel used by farm machinery in crop cultivation, things that aggravate climate change.

Livestock grazing has other noteworthy environmental benefits as well. Compared to cropland, perennial pastures used for grazing can decrease soil erosion by 80 percent and markedly improve water quality, Minnesota's Land Stewardship Project research has found. Even the United Nations report acknowledges, "There is growing evidence that both cattle ranching and pastoralism can have positive impacts on biodiversity."

As the contrast between the environmental impact of traditional farming and industrial farming shows, efforts to minimize greenhouse gases need to be much more sophisticated than just making blanket condemnations of certain foods. Farming methods vary tremendously, leading to widely variable global warming contributions for every food we eat. Recent research in Sweden shows that, depending on how and where a food is produced, its carbon dioxide emissions vary by a factor of 10.

And it should also be noted that farmers bear only a portion of the blame for greenhouse gas emissions in the food system. Only about one-fifth of the food system's energy use is farm-related, according to University of Wisconsin research. And the Soil Association in Britain estimates that only half of food's total greenhouse impact has any connection to farms. The rest comes from processing, transportation, storage, retailing and food preparation. The seemingly innocent potato chip, for instance, turns out to be a dreadfully climate-hostile food. Foods that are minimally processed, in season and locally grown, like those available at farmers' markets and backyard gardens, are generally the most climate-friendly.

Rampant waste at the processing, retail and household stages compounds the problem. About half of the food produced in the United States is thrown away, according to University of Arizona research. Thus, a consumer could measurably reduce personal global warming impact simply by more judicious grocery purchasing and use.

None of us, whether we are vegan or omnivore, can entirely avoid foods that play a role in global warming. Singling out meat is misleading and unhelpful, especially since few people are likely to entirely abandon animal-based foods. Mr. Gore, for one, apparently has no intention of going vegan. The 90 percent of Americans who eat meat and dairy are likely to respond the same way.

Still, there are numerous reasonable ways to reduce our individual contributions to climate change through our food choices. Because it takes more resources to produce meat and dairy than, say, fresh locally grown carrots, it's sensible to cut back on consumption of animal-based foods. More important, all eaters can lower their global warming contribution by following these simple rules: avoid processed foods and those from industrialized farms; reduce food waste; and buy local and in season.

Not all meat is created equal, Niman argues in her op-ed piece. Instead of condemning all meat, Niman claims that industrial farming produces markedly more carbon dioxide, methane, and nitrous oxides than traditional farming and ranching. She and her husband, Bill Niman, formerly owned Niman Ranch and currently own BN Ranch. Research the farming techniques of each ranch. Why did the Nimans leave Niman Ranch? How do the operations of BN Ranch differ?

Many authors in this collection—Wendell Berry, Joel Salatin, and even Nicolette Niman—work to condense complex food problems into memorable eating rules. But, as Niman argues, sometimes these well-intentioned efforts "need to be much more sophisticated than just making blanket condemnations of certain foods." Do you think that there are universal food rules of how we should produce and eat food? Or are such rules by definition reductive and unable to capture each individual's situation?

What's your carbon footprint? Find a carbon footprint calculator online (one can be found at *www.nature.org/initiatives/climatechange/calculator/*) and asses your carbon impact. As a class, post your results on a blog. Write individual entries describing your results. Are you surprised by your findings? Were you expecting the questions presented? Did you find ideas to reduce your carbon footprint? In addition, respond to fellow classmates' entries.

FOOD

Joel Salatin is a third-generation alternative farmer at Polyface Farm in Virginia's Shenandoah Valley. He and his farm have been featured in several national publications, in Michael Pollan's book The Omnivore's Dilemma, *and in the documentary film* Food, Inc. *Salatin wrote this essay for* Food, Inc.: How Industrial Food Is Making Us Sicker, Fatter, and Poorer—*and* What You Can Do about It, *the companion book to that film.*

DECLARE YOUR INDEPENDENCE

By Joel Salatin

Perhaps the most empowering concept in any paradigm-challenging movement is simply opting out. The opt-out strategy can humble the mightiest forces because it declares to one and all, "You do not control me."

The time has come for people who are ready to challenge the paradigm of factory-produced food and to return to a more natural, wholesome, and sustainable way of eating (and living) to make that declaration to the powers that be, in business and government, that established the existing system and continue to prop it up. It's time to opt out and simply start eating better—right here, right now.

Impractical? Idealistic? Utopian? Not really. As I'll explain, it's actually the most realistic and effective approach to transforming a system that is slowly but surely killing us.

WHAT HAPPENED TO FOOD?

First, why am I taking a position that many well-intentioned people might consider alarmist or extreme? Let me explain.

At the risk of stating the obvious, the unprecedented variety of bar-coded packages in today's supermarket really does not mean that our generation enjoys better food options than our predecessors. These packages, by and large, having passed through the food inspection fraternity, the industrial food fraternity, and the lethargic cheap-food-purchasing consumer fraternity, represent an incredibly narrow choice. If you took away everything with an ingredient foreign to our three trillion intestinal microflora, the shelves would be bare indeed. (I'm talking here about the incredible variety of microorganisms that live in our digestive tracts and perform an array of useful functions, including training our immune systems and producing vitamins like biotin and vitamin K.) In fact, if you just eliminated every product that would have been unavailable in 1900, almost everything would be gone, including staples that had been chemically fertilized, sprayed with pesticides, or ripened with gas.

Rather than representing newfound abundance, these packages wending their way to store shelves after spending a month in the belly of Chinese merchant marines are actually the meager offerings of a tyrannical food system. Strong words? Try buying real milk—as in raw. See if you can find meat processed in the clean open air under sterilizing sunshine. Look for pot pies made with local produce and meat. How about good old unpasteurized apple cider? Fresh cheese? Unpasteurized almonds? All these staples that our great-grandparents relished and grew healthy on have been banished from today's supermarkets.

They've been replaced by an array of pseudo-foods that did not exist a mere century ago. The food additives, preservatives, colorings, emulsifiers, corn syrups, and unpronounceable ingredients listed on the colorful packages bespeak a centralized control mindset that actually reduces the options available to fill Americans' dinner plates. Whether by intentional design or benign ignorance, the result has been the same—the criminalization and/or demonization of heritage foods.

The mindset behind this radical transformation of American eating habits expresses itself in at least a couple of ways.

One is the completely absurd argument that without industrial food, the world would starve. "How can you feed the world?" is the most common question people ask me when they tour Polyface Farm. Actually, when you consider the fact that millions of people, including many vast cities, were fed and sustained using traditional farming methods until just a few decades ago, the answer is obvious. America has traded seventy-five million buffalo, which required no tillage, petroleum, or chemicals, for a mere forty-two million head of cattle. Even with all the current chemical inputs, our production is a shadow of what it was 500 years ago. Clearly, if we returned to herbivorous principles five centuries old, we could double our meat supply. The potential for similar increases exists for other food items.

The second argument is about food safety. "How can we be sure that food produced on local farms without centralized inspection and processing is really safe to eat?" Here, too, the facts are opposite to what many people assume. The notion that indigenous food is unsafe simply has no scientific backing. Milk-borne pathogens, for example, became a significant health problem only during a narrow time period between 1900 and 1930, before refrigeration but after unprecedented urban expansion. Breweries needed to be located near metropolitan centers, and adjacent dairies fed herbivore-unfriendly brewery waste to cows. The combination created real problems that do not exist in grass-based dairies practicing good sanitation under refrigeration conditions.

Lest you think the pressure to maintain the industrialized food system is all really about food safety, consider that all the natural-food items I listed above can be given away, and the donors are considered pillars of community benevolence. But as soon as money changes hands, all these wonderful choices become "hazardous substances," guaranteed to send our neighbors to the hospital with food poisoning. Maybe it's not human health but corporate profits that are really being protected.

Furthermore, realize that many of the same power brokers (politicians and the like) encourage citizens to go out into the woods on a 70-degree fall day; gut-shoot a deer with possible variant Creutzfeld-Jacob's disease (like mad cow for deer); drag the carcass a mile through squirrel dung, sticks, and rocks; then drive parade-like through town in the blazing afternoon sun with the carcass prominently displayed on the hood of the Blazer. The hunter takes the carcass home, strings it up in the backyard tree under roosting birds for a week, then skins it out and feeds the meat to his children. This is all considered noble and wonderful, even patriotic. Safety? It's not an issue.

The question is, who decides what food is safe? In our society, the decisions are made by the same type of people who decided in the Dred Scott ruling that slaves were not human beings. Just because well-educated, credentialed experts say something does not make it true. History abounds with expert opinion that turned out to be dead wrong. Ultimately, food safety is a personal matter of choice, of conscience. In fact, if high-fructose corn syrup is hazardous to health—and certainly we could argue that it is—then half of the government-sanctioned food in supermarkets is unsafe. Mainline soft drinks would carry a warning label. Clearly, safety is a subjective matter.

RECLAIMING FOOD FREEDOM

Once we realize that safety is a matter of personal choice, individual freedom suddenly—and appropriately—takes center stage. What could be a more basic freedom than the freedom to choose what to feed my three-trillion-member internal community?

In America I have the freedom to own guns, speak, and assemble. But what good are those freedoms if I can't choose to eat what my body wants in order to have the energy to shoot, preach, and worship? The only reason the framers of the American Constitution and Bill of Rights did not guarantee freedom of food choice was that they couldn't envision a day when neighbor-to-neighbor commerce would be criminalized...when the bureaucratic-industrial food fraternity would subsidize corn syrup and create a nation of diabetes sufferers, but deny my neighbor a pound of sausage from my Thanksgiving hog killin'.

People tend to have short memories. We all assume that whatever is must be normal. Industrial food is not normal. Nothing about it is normal. In the continuum of human history, what western civilization has done to its food in the last century represents a mere blip. It is a grand experiment on an ever-widening global scale. We have not been here before. The three trillion members of our intestinal community have not been here before. If we ate like humans have eaten for as long as anyone has kept historical records, almost nothing in the supermarket would be on the table.

A reasonable person, looking at the lack of choice we now suffer, would ask for a Food Emancipation Proclamation. Food has been enslaved by so-called inspectors that deem the most local, indigenous, heritage-based, and traditional foods unsafe and make them illegal. It has been enslaved by a host-consuming agricultural parasite called "government farm subsidies." It has been enslaved by corporate-subsidized research that declared for four decades that feeding dead cows to cows was sound science—until mad cows came to dinner.

The same criminalization is occurring on the production side. The province of Quebec has virtually outlawed outdoor poultry. Ponds, which stabilize hydrologic cycles and have forever been considered natural assets, are now considered liabilities because they encourage wild birds, which could bring avian influenza. And with the specter of a National Animal Identification System being rammed down farmers' throats, small flocks and herds are being economized right out of existence.

On our Polyface Farm nestled in Virginia's Shenandoah Valley, we have consciously opted out of the industrial production and marketing paradigms. Meat chickens move every day in floorless, portable shelters across the pasture, enjoying bugs, forage, and local grain (grown free of genetically modified organisms). Tyson-style, inhumane, fecal factory chicken houses have no place here.

The magical land-healing process we use, with cattle using mob-stocking, herbivorous, solar conversion, lignified carbon sequestration fertilization, runs opposite the grain-based feedlot system practiced by mainline industrial cattle production. We move the cows every day from paddock to paddock, allowing the forage to regenerate completely through its growth curve, metabolizing solar energy into biomass.

Our pigs aerate anaerobic, fermented bedding in the hay feeding shed, where manure, carbon, and corn create a pig delight. We actually believe that honoring and respecting the "pigness" of the pig is the first step in an ethical, moral cultural code. By contrast, today's industrial food system views pigs as merely inanimate piles of protoplasmic molecular structure to be manipulated with whatever cleverness the egocentric human mind can conceive. A society that views its plants and animals from that manipulative, egocentric, mechanistic mindset will soon come to view its citizens in the same way. How we respect and honor the least of these is how we respect and honor the greatest of these.

The industrial pig growers are even trying to find the stress gene so it can be taken out of the pig's DNA. That way the pigs can be abused but won't be stressed about it. Then they can be crammed in even tighter quarters without cannibalizing and getting sick. In the name of all that's decent, what kind of ethics encourages such notions?

In just the last couple of decades, Americans have learned a new lexicon of squiggly Latin words: camphylobacter, lysteria, E. coli, salmonella, bovine spongiform encephalopathy, avian influenza. Whence these strange words? Nature is speaking a protest, screaming to our generation: "Enough!" The assault on biological dignity has pushed nature to the limit. Begging for mercy, its pleas go largely unheeded on Wall Street, where Conquistadors subjugating weaker species think they can forever tyrannize without an eventual payback. But the rapist will pay—eventually. You and I must bring a nurturing mentality to the table to balance the industrial food mindset.

Here at Polyface, eggmobiles follow the cows through the grazing cycle. These portable laying hen trailers allow the birds to scratch through the cows' dung and harvest newly uncovered crickets and grasshoppers, acting like a biological pasture sanitizer. This biomimicry stands in stark contrast to chickens housed beak by wattle in egg factories, never allowed to see sunshine or chase a grasshopper.

We have done all of this without money or encouragement from those who hold the reins of food power, government or private. We haven't asked for grants. We haven't asked for permission. In fact, to the shock and amazement of our urban friends, our farm is considered a Typhoid Mary by our industrial farm neighbors. Why? Because we don't medicate, vaccinate, genetically adulterate, irradiate, or exudate like they do. They fear our methods because they've been conditioned by the powers that be to fear our methods.

The point of all this is that if anyone waits for credentialed industrial experts, whether government or nongovernement, to create ecologically, nutritionally, and emotionally friendly food, they might as well get ready for a long, long wait. For example, just imagine what a grass-finished herbivore paradigm would do to the financial and power structure of America. Today, roughly seventy percent of all grains go through herbivores, which aren't supposed to eat them and, in nature, never do. If the land devoted to that production were converted to perennial prairie polycultures under indigenous biomimicry management, it would topple the grain cartel and reduce petroleum usage, chemical usage, machinery manufacture, and bovine pharmaceuticals.

Think about it. That's a lot of economic inertia resisting change. Now do you see why the Farm Bill that controls government input into our agricultural system never changes by more than about two percent every few years? Even so-called conservation measures usually end up serving the power brokers when all is said and done.

OPTING OUT

If things are going to change, it is up to you and me to make the change. But what is the most efficacious way to make the change? Is it through legislation? Is it by picketing the World Trade Organization talks? Is it by dumping cow manure on the parking lot at McDonald's? Is it by demanding regulatory restraint over the aesthetically and aromatically repulsive industrial food system?

At the risk of being labeled simplistic, I suggest that the most efficacious way to change things is simply to declare our independence from the figurative kings in the industrial system. To make the point clear, here at the hallmarks of the industrial food system:

- Centralized production
- Mono-speciation
- Genetic manipulation
- Centralized processing
- Confined animal feeding operations
- Things that end in "cide" (Latin for death)
- Ready-to-Eat food
- Long-distance transportation
- Externalized costs—economy, society, ecology
- Pharmaceuticals
- Opaqueness
- Unpronounceable ingredients
- Supermarkets
- Fancy packaging
- High fructose corn syrup
- High liability insurance
- "No Trespassing" signs

Reviewing this list shows the magnitude and far-reaching power of the industrial food system. I contend that it will not move. Entrenched paradigms never move...until outside forces move them. And those forces always come from the bottom up. The people who sit on the throne tend to like things the way they are. They have no reason to change until they are forced to do so.

The most powerful force you and I can exert on the system is to opt out. Just declare that we will not participate. Resistance movements from the antislavery movement to women's suffrage to sustainable agriculture always have and always will begin with opt-out resistance to the status quo. And seldom does an issue present itself with such a daily—in fact, thrice daily—opportunity to opt out.

Perhaps the best analogy in recent history is the home-school movement. In the late 1970s, as more families began opting out of institutional educational settings, credentialed educational experts warned us about the jails and mental asylums we'd have to build to handle the educationally and socially deprived children that home-schooling would produce. Many parents went to jail for violating school truancy laws. A quarter-century later, of course, the paranoid predictions are universally recognized as wrong. Not everyone opts for home-schooling, but the option must be available for those who want it. In the same way, an opt-out food movement will eventually show the Henny Penny food police just how wrong they are.

LEARN TO COOK AGAIN

I think the opt-out strategy involves at least four basic ideas.

First, we must rediscover our kitchens. Never has a culture spent more to remodel and techno-glitz its kitchens, but at the same time been more lost as to where the kitchen is and what it's for. As a culture, we don't cook any more. Americans consume nearly a quarter of all their food in their cars, for crying out loud. Americans graze through the kitchen, popping precooked, heat-and-eat, bar-coded packages into the microwave for eating-on-the-run.

That treatment doesn't work with real food. Real heritage food needs to be sliced, peeled, sautéed, marinated, puréed, and a host of other things that require true culinary skills. Back in the early 1980s when our farm began selling pastured poultry, nobody even asked for boneless, skinless breast. To be perfectly sexist, every mom knew how to cut up a chicken. That was generic cultural mom information. Today, half of the moms don't know that a chicken even has bones.

I was delivering to one of our buying club drops a couple of months ago, and one of the ladies discreetly pulled me aside and asked: "How do you make a hamburger?" I thought I'd misunderstood, and asked her to repeat the question. I bent my ear down close to hear her sheepishly repeat the same question. I looked at her incredulously and asked: "Are you kidding?"

"My husband and I have been vegetarians. But now that we realize we can save the world by eating grass-based livestock, we're eating meat, and he wants a hamburger. But I don't know how to make it." This was an upper-middle-income, college-educated, bright, intelligent woman.

The indigenous knowledge base surrounding food is largely gone. When "scratch" cooking means actually opening a can, and when church and family reunion potlucks include buckets of Kentucky Fried Chicken, you know our culture has suffered a culinary information implosion. Big time. Indeed, according to marketing surveys roughly seventy percent of Americans have no idea what they are having for supper at 4:00 p.m. That's scary.

Whatever happened to planning the week's menus? We still do that at our house. In the summer, our Polyface interns and apprentices enjoy creating a potluck for all of us Salatins every Saturday evening. All week they connive to plan the meal. It develops throughout the week, morphs into what is available locally and seasonally, and always culminates in a fellowship feast.

As a culture, if all we did was rediscover our kitchens and quit buying prepared foods, it would fundamentally change the industrial food system. The reason I'm leading this discussion with that option is because too often the foodies and greenies seem to put the onus for change on the backs of farmers. But this is a team effort, and since farmers do not even merit Census Bureau recognition, non-farmers must ante up to the responsibility for the change. And both moms and dads need to reclaim the basic food preparation knowledge that was once the natural inheritance of every human being.

BUY LOCAL

After rediscovering your kitchen, the next opt-out strategy is to purchase as directly as possible from your local farmer. If the money pouring into industrial food dried up tomorrow, that system would cease to exist. Sounds easy, doesn't it? Actually, it is. It doesn't take any legislation, regulation, taxes, agencies, or programs. As the money flows to local producers, more producers will join them. The only reason the local food system is still minuscule is because few people patronize it.

Even organics have been largely co-opted by industrial systems. Go to a food co-op drop, and you'll find that more than half the dollars are being spent for organic corn chips, treats, and snacks. From far away.

Just for fun, close your eyes and imagine walking down the aisle of your nearby Wal-Mart or Whole Foods. Make a note of each item as you walk by and think about what could be grown within one hundred miles of that venue. I recommend this exercise when speaking at conferences all over the world, and it's astounding the effect it has on people. As humans, we tend to get mired in the sheer monstrosity of it all. But if we break it down into little bits, suddenly the job seems doable. Can milk be produced within one hundred miles of you? Eggs? Tomatoes? Why not?

Not everything can be grown locally, but the lion's shares of what you eat certainly can. I was recently in the San Joaquin Valley looking at almonds—square miles of almonds. Some eighty-five percent of all the world's almonds are grown in that area. Why not grow a variety of things for the people of Los Angeles instead? My goodness, if you're going to irrigate anyway, why not grow things that will be eaten locally rather than things that will be shipped to some far corner of the world? Why indeed? Because most people aren't asking for local. Los Angeles is buying peas from China so almonds can be shipped to China.

Plenty of venues exist for close exchange to happen. Farmers' markets are a big and growing part of this movement. They provide a social atmosphere and a wide variety of fare. Too often; however, their politics and regulations stifle vendors. And they aren't open every day for the convenience of shoppers.

Community-supported agriculture (CSA) is a shared-risk investment that answers some of the tax and liability issues surrounding food commerce. Patrons invest in a portion of the farm's products and receive a share every week during the season. The drawback is the paperwork and lack of patron choice.

Food boutiques or niche retail facades are gradually filling a necessary role because most farmers' markets are not open daily. The price markup may be more, but the convenience is real. These allow farmers to drop off products quickly and go back to farming or other errands. Probably the biggest challenge with these venues is their overhead relative to scale.

Farmgate sales, especially near cities, are wonderful retail opportunities. Obviously, traveling to the farm has its drawbacks, but actually visiting the farm creates an accountability and transparency that are hard to achieve in any other venue. To acquire food on the farmer's own turf creates a connection, relationship, and memory that heighten the intimate dining experience. The biggest hurdle is zoning laws that often do not allow neighbors to collaboratively sell. (My book *Everything I Want to Do Is Illegal* details the local food hurdles in greater detail.)

Metropolitan buying clubs (MBCs) are developing rapidly as a new local marketing and distribution venue. Using the Internet as a farmer-to-patron real-time communication avenue, this scheme offers scheduled drops in urban areas. Patrons order via the Internet from an inventory supplied by one or more farms. Drop points in their neighborhoods offer easy access. Farmers do not have farmers' market politics or regulations to deal with, or sales commissions to pay. This transaction is highly efficient because it is nonspeculative—everything that goes on the delivery vehicle is preordered, and nothing comes back to the farm. Customizing each delivery's inventory for seasonal availability offers flexibility and an info-dense menu.

Many people ask, "Where do I find local food, or a farmer?" My answer: "They are all around. If you will put as much time into sourcing your local food as many people put into picketing and political posturing, you will discover a whole world that Wall Street doesn't know exists." I am a firm believer in the Chinese proverb: "When the student is ready, the teacher will appear." This nonindustrial food system lurks below the radar in every locality. If you seek, you will find.

BUY WHAT'S IN SEASON

After discovering your kitchen and finding your farmer, the third opt-out procedure is to eat seasonally. This includes "laying by" for the off season. Eating seasonally does not mean denying yourself tomatoes in January if you live in New Hampshire. It means procuring the mountains of late-season tomatoes thrown away each year and canning, freezing, or dehydrating them for winter use.

In our basement, hundreds of quarts of canned summer produce line the pantry shelves. Green beans, yellow squash, applesauce, pickled beets, pickles, relish, and a host of other delicacies await off-season menus. I realize this takes time, but it's the way for all of us to share bioregional rhythms. To refuse to join this natural food ebb and flow is to deny connectedness. And this indifference to life around us creates a jaundiced view of our ecological nest and our responsibilities within it.

For the first time in human history, a person can move into a community, build a house out of outsourced material, heat it with outsourced energy, hook up to water from an unknown source, send waste out a pipe somewhere else, and eat food from an unknown source. In other words, in modern America we can live without any regard to the ecological life raft that undergirds us. Perhaps that is why many of us have become indifferent to nature's cry.

The most unnatural characteristic of the industrial food system is the notion that the same food items should be available everywhere at once at all times. To have empty grocery shelves during inventory downtime is unthinkable in the supermarket world. When we refuse to participate in the nonseasonal game, it strikes a heavy blow to the infrastructure, pipeline, distribution system, and ecological assault that upholds industrial food.

PLANT A GARDEN

My final recommendation for declaring your food independence is to grow some of your own. I am constantly amazed at the creativity shown by urban-dwellers who physically embody their opt-out decision by growing something themselves. For some, it may be a community garden where neighbors work together to grow tomatoes, beans, and squash. For others, it may be three or four laying hens in an apartment. Shocking? Why? As a culture, we think nothing of having exotic tropical birds in city apartments. Why not use that space for something productive, like egg layers? Feed them kitchen scraps and gather fresh eggs every day.

Did someone mention something about ordinances? Forget them. Do it anyway. Defy. Don't comply. People who think nothing of driving around Washington, D.C., at eighty miles an hour in a fifty-five speed limit zone often go apoplectic at the thought of defying a zoning or building-code ordinance. The secret reality is that the government is out of money and can't hire enough bureaucrats to check up on everybody anyway. So we all need to just begin opting out and it will be like five lanes of speeders on the beltway—who do you stop?

Have you ever wanted to have a cottage business producing that wonderful soup, pot pie, or baked item your grandmother used to make? Well, go ahead and make it, sell it to your neighbors and friends at church or garden club. Food safety laws? Forget them. People getting sick from food aren't getting it from their neighbors; they are getting it from USDA-approved, industrially produced, irradiated, amalgamated, adulterated, reconstituted, extruded, pseudo-food laced with preservatives, dyes, and high fructose corn syrup.

If you live in a condominium complex, approach the landlord about taking over a patch for a garden. Plant edible landscaping. If all the campuses in Silicon Valley would plant edible varieties instead of high-maintenance ornamentals, their irrigation water would actually be put to ecological use instead of just feeding hedge clippers and lawn mower engines. Urban garden projects are taking over abandoned lots, and that is a good thing. We need to see more of that. Schools can produce their own food. Instead of hiring Chemlawn, how about running pastured poultry across the yard? Students can butcher the chickens and learn about the death-life-death-life cycle.

Clearly, so much can be done right here, right now, with what you and I have. The question is not, "What can I force someone else to do?" The question is "What am I doing today to opt out of the industrial food system?" For some, it may be having one family sit-down, locally-sourced meal a week. That's fine. We haven't gotten where we've gotten overnight, and we certainly won't extract ourselves from where we are overnight.

But we must stop feeling like victims and adopt a proactive stance. The power of many individual right actions will then compound to create a different culture. Our children deserve it. And the earthworms will love us—along with the rest of the planet.

"As a culture, we don't cook anymore," Salatin writes in his essay. "We need to rediscover our kitchens." Reread the section titled "Learn to Cook Again" and, with the principles Salatin states in mind, plan a meal you could cook using your own kitchen (or whatever available means you have to cook). Start by seeking out recipes and local ingredients (you might interview family members for the former and visit a local farmer's market for the latter). Then, plan your meal and prepare a menu and explanation of how the meal fits Salatin's ideas about leaving the industrial food system behind.

How does Salatin address the two major concerns he mentions about his proposal—that the world will not be able to feed itself without industrial food and that locally grown food is not always safe? Do you think his handling of these concerns is sufficient?

Write a formal letter to Salatin in which you raise any questions you have about his proposal—about its feasibility, for example, or its effectiveness.

As a class or with a small group, compare Wendell Berry's 1989 "The Pleasures of Eating" (which begins on page 21) with Salatin's 2009 "Declare Your Independence." How have arguments in the food revolution changed over the past two decades? Do you think the arguments have shifted dramatically since 1989? What similarities do you see between the two pieces?

MAJOR ASSIGNMENTS

MAJOR ASSIGNMENT #1:
WRITING A FOOD MEMOIR

BACKGROUND

Several authors in this book write intimate accounts of what food, cooking, and eating mean to them—from Wendell Berry's ode to the pleasures of eating to Julie Powell's culinary adventures inspired by Julia Child. No matter the author or the topic, these pieces use personal experience related in narrative fashion to connect with an audience; in other words, they tell private stories to make public points about a variety of food-related subjects.

ASSIGNMENT

First, read a few—if not all—of the pieces by Berry, Powell, David Sedaris, Jessica B. Harris, and Anthony Bourdain. Then, using these as a jumping off point, write a memoir essay that uses thoughtful plotting, vivid description, and character development to tell a compelling story about one significant food-related moment, memory, or theme drawn from your life. Base your memoir on an experience that left a lasting impression on you and that you can use to speak to your audience.

QUESTIONS FOR INVENTION

After you have decided on your topic, think about the following questions:

- What specific message do you want to convey about your food-related experience? (In other words, what is your purpose in writing about this particular experience or event?)

- What kind of reaction do you want from your audience? What do you want them to take from your essay?

- What is the best way to connect with your audience? (Think, for example, about the things you want your audience to see, hear, smell, taste, and feel about your subject.)

ABOUT MEMOIR ESSAYS

A memoir is a kind of personal essay in which the writer uses selected life experiences to connect with and convey a larger message to the audience. As you brainstorm and begin drafting your essay, keep in mind that a memoir should:

- Focus on a slice of your life, rather than your entire life, to convey a specific message and/or emotion to the audience

- Explore your memory of the experience, using narratives (or stories), to explain its significance to the audience

- Include concrete details that appeal to the audience's senses

- Reflect on the experience to help the audience understand how it affected you and why it should matter to them.

ASSIGNMENTS

MAJOR ASSIGNMENT #2:
ANALYZING A LOCAL RESTAURANT MENU

BACKGROUND

In the early 1980s Alice Waters made history by including the first proper-noun meat on a menu: Niman Ranch beef. Since then, local- and artisanal-minded chefs have followed suit to indicate their commitment to the ideals of a loosely defined food revolution. Finding a chef's eating or food philosophy isn't just reserved for idealists. Even fast food restaurants demonstrate their beliefs through menu design. For instance, McDonalds boasts "Extra Value Meals" and a "Dollar Menu," indicating its appeal to cost consciousness.

ASSIGNMENT

Write an essay in which you analyze a local restaurant's menu and reveal its eating or food philosophy. Break apart the visual and textual elements of the menu in order to find out the force of its appeal to customers. Your objective is to analyze how and what the menu is persuading you to think about eating or food. You should argue a link between specific rhetorical choices on the menu and their effects.

RESEARCH AND INVENTION QUESTIONS

The following questions will help you get started:

- What is the name of the restaurant? What type of cuisine does it offer? Is it a chain restaurant? Is it a themed restaurant?

- What kind of reputation does the restaurant have? Are there elements on the menu that support or undermine that reputation?

- Who are the customers? Who is the restaurant's target demographic?

- What assumptions does the menu make about your values or beliefs? How do these assumptions show up in the menu?

- How much writing is on the menu? On what does the writing focus? Are there descriptions of how dishes are prepared? Does the menu include where the food comes from?

- Are there any images on the menu? If so, what do they look like? Where are the images placed?

- How would you describe the tone, style, and emotion of the menu? Is it playful? Serious? Succinct? Verbose? Accessible? Difficult to understand? How does the menu achieve its effect?

- Where was the food on the menu produced? How was it produced? When necessary, ask the restaurant's manager for supporting details.

- What story does the menu tell about how food should be eaten? Is eating about having fun? Connecting with friends and family? Fueling the body? Supporting local economies? Sustaining the environment? Saving money? Enjoying an unmatched experience? Be sure to link the menu's philosophy with concrete visual and textual details of the menu.

MAJOR ASSIGNMENT #3:
PERSUADING AMERICANS TO COOK (OR NOT)

BACKGROUND

Wendell Berry and Joel Salatin mourn the decline of real scratch cooking—that is, composing a meal from non-processed foods. Not only do they see home cooking as healthier than diets heavy in processed foods, but they also laud cooking as a forgotten pleasure and a vehicle for empowerment. Other writers agree. Julie Powell discovers the life-changing possibilities in potato soup; Anthony Bourdain finds power in an oyster; and Mario Batali playfully teases dinner party guests with his succulent *lardo*.

ASSIGNMENT

Take the cooking challenge these essays suggest. Is cooking from scratch the radical experience these authors describe? In groups, compose a series of short videos to be posted on *YouTube*, documenting your experiences and conveying your cooking perspective. Take viewers on your adventure from shopping, to deciding on a menu, to cooking, to eating. The video series should encourage your audience to view cooking in a particular way. More than simply documenting a series of acts, you should consciously create a point of view on cooking. Should we go back to a Julia Child-inspired era or are we better off leaving the cooking to the professionals?

RESEARCH AND INVENTION QUESTIONS

These questions are designed to help you plan your video:

- What specific message do you want to convey with your video? Is food preparation a pleasure or anxiety-inducing endeavor? Is it worth the time and effort?

- What kind of reaction do you want from your audience? What feelings do you want your audience to take from your video? What visual elements can you implement to achieve your desired effects?

- Watch a few food-related shows. Try some of the shows on Food Network or click over to Food Network's new sister station, the Cooking channel. You might even catch some old episodes of Julia Child's The French Chef. What patterns do you observe in terms of cooking and shopping locations, story organization, camera angles, music, and lighting? Which of these strategies can you use in your production?

ABOUT FOOD VIDEOS

Although many food videos are designed to look casual and improvised, there's often a great deal of preparation to achieve this effect. Plan and practice your video before you record. Write a loose script from which you can build and improvise. Edit your footage to achieve a desired effect. Finally, be sure to leave your viewers with a strong sense of your cooking perspective.

MAJOR ASSIGNMENT #4:
EXPLAINING A FOOD PRODUCTION TECHNIQUE

BACKGROUND

"Fear Factories" by Matthew Scully takes readers into the world of modern food production by explaining how inhumane factory-farming practices dominate the industrial food system. Scully's essay harkens back to Wendell Berry's encouragement in "The Pleasures of Eating" to stay informed about how our food is produced. Knowing the techniques of farming and food production, for Berry, safeguards consumers from unhealthy and unethical purchases.

ASSIGNMENT

With these ideas in mind, this assignment asks you to research and explain an agricultural or food production technique to an audience of potential consumers. Select a technique or process that interests you and conduct research to learn as much as you can about it. Then, write an essay in which you explain the technique to an audience unfamiliar with it. As you consider a topic, think broadly about both industrial and traditional food production practices. You may select an antiquated farming technique that is no longer practical or a nascent industrial technology. Whatever you decide, your goal is to help your readers understand your topic as well as you do after you have conducted your research.

Keep in mind that you're not writing an essay that expresses your opinion or position on the practice (in other words, you are not writing a Berry-style judgment on the farming technique). Your focus should be presenting a clear and accurate explanation of the process you have chosen.

RESEARCH

Your instructor will give you more details about the kind of research you should do as you prepare to write your essay—and may ask you to compile an annotated bibliography of sources as an invention exercise. In general, you should consider sources that can help you:

- Understand and convey to your audience relevant background about your topic. What, for example, do you need to learn and share with your audience in order to prepare them for the explanation to come?

- Make your readers care about the topic. This is especially important if you think your audience might be hostile, skeptical, or apathetic about the farming technique you plan to explain. What can you share with your readers to make them want to read what you have to say?

- Explain the process or technique to your readers. Do you need data, statistics, or other "hard" information to help explain your topic? Do you need expertise from people or sources more knowledgeable about the topic than you? Do you need to include images of some kind? In your paper, you'll need to explain how and why the technique was developed; what it is used for and who is or was using it; how it works; and any controversy surrounding it.

MAJOR ASSIGNMENT #5:
PROPOSING A ROLE FOR GOVERNMENT IN AGRICULTURE

BACKGROUND

Several authors in the readings reference the dawn of industrial agriculture after World War II as the beginning of an agricultural Dark Age. Together, the pieces by Wendell Berry, Alice Waters, Eliot Coleman, Matthew Scully, Nicolette Hahn Niman, and Joel Salatin see the American food system, with the government's blessing, as abandoning hard working individuals attuned to the natural cycles of the environment in favor of big businesses whose primary goal is increased revenue. By contrast, Robert Paarlberg, in "Attention Whole Foods Shoppers," praises the current system for allowing more affordable and safer food options. This assignment asks you to weigh in on this issue.

ASSIGNMENT

Write a policy argument in which you comment on how you view this change. Has the government's reconfiguration of the food system been mostly beneficial or harmful? By what standards should we base our judgments? Based on the reading you've done in this book, on class discussions, and on library and online research, write an argument proposing what the government's role should be in the current agricultural landscape. Your goal in this text is to persuade the audience to your way of thinking about your topic and, perhaps, to move them to action. To do these things, you will have to:

- Make your audience care about the topic.

- Find ways to appeal to your audience emotionally and intellectually.

- Be clear about your position and about what, if anything, you want your audience to do.

- Provide ample evidence to persuade the audience that your position is reasonable and worthy of their consideration.

- Address opposing positions.

RESEARCH QUESTIONS

Your instructor will give you more details about the kind of research you should do as you prepare to write your essay—and may ask you to compile an annotated bibliography of sources as an invention exercise. In general, you should consider sources that can help you:

- Understand and convey to your audience relevant background about your topic. What, for example, do you need to learn and share with your audience in order to support your proposal?

- Contextualize your topic. Where do things stand with the current food system? What are the arguments for and against current government subsidies? What does it cost (financially and environmentally) to maintain the current system?

- Make your readers care about the topic. This is especially important if you think your audience might be hostile, skeptical, or apathetic about the current food system. What can you share with your readers to make them want to read what you have to say?

- Identify and address positions that oppose your own. Who disagrees with your position and why? Why should readers not be convinced by opposing arguments? What makes your position stronger?

FILMOGRAPHY

DOCUMENTARIES

Most films that deal directly with food-related issues are, not surprisingly, documentaries. And many of these focus on the globalized industrial food system and the heavy toll it takes on people, animals, and the environment.

THE INDUSTRIAL FOOD SYSTEM... AND ALTERNATIVES

As We Sow
Black Gold
Death on a Factory Farm
Dirt: The Movie
Food Beware: The French Organic Revolution
Food, Inc.
Food Fight
Food Stamped
Fresh
The Future of Food
Good Food
King Corn
Our Daily Bread
The Price of Sugar
We Feed the World
What's on Your Plate?

FOOD AND HEALTH

Diet for a New America
Food Matters

Killer at Large
Processed People
Super Size Me

FOOD AND PEOPLE
All in This Tea
American Dream
Eat This New York
Friday's at the Farm
The Garden
Hamburger America
It's Grits
The Kings of Pastry
The Lunch Line
Pressure Cooker
The Real Dirt on Farmer John
Yum, Yum, Yum!

FEATURE FILMS

While many feature films include food-related plotlines, we've listed a handful in which food and/or food production, consumption, culture, and identity have a starring role, so to speak.
Babette's Feast
Big Night
Eat Drink Man Woman
Fast Food Nation
Julie and Julia
Kitchen Stories
Mostly Martha
Sideways
Soul Food
Tampopo
The Milagro Beanfield War
Waitress

WORKS CITED

"Angelica Kitchen." http://www.angelicakitchen.com. Angelica Kitchen 2008. Web. 11 Oct. 2010.

Berry, Wendell. "The Pleasures of Eating." *What Are People For?* New York: North Point Press, 2000. 145-152. Print.

Bourdain, Anthony. "Food is Good." *Kitchen Confidential: Adventures in the Culinary Underbelly.* New York: Bloomsbury, USA, 2000. 9-18. Print.

Bourdain, Anthony. "Who Cooks?" *Kitchen Confidential: Adventures in the Culinary Underbelly.* New York: Bloomsbury, USA, 2000. 55-63. Print.

Buford, Bill. "Dinner With Mario." *Heat: An Amateur's Adventures as Kitchen Slave, Line Cook, Pasta-Maker, and Apprentice to a Dante-Quoting Butcher in Tuscany.* New York: Knopf Doubleday, 2007. 1-10. Print.

Catacalos, Renee Brooks & Kristi Bahrenburg Janzen. "Suburban Foraging: Two Families Eat Only Local." *Mother Earth News* 217 (Aug./Sept. 2006): n. pag. Web. 11 Oct. 2010.

Coleman, Eliot. "Beyond Organic." *Mother Earth News* 189 (Dec./Jan. 2002): n. pag. Web. 11 Oct. 2010.

Dahm, Molly J., et al. "Organic Foods: Do Eco-Friendly Attitudes Predict Eco-Friendly Behaviors?" *Journal of American College Health* 58.3 (Nov./ Dec. 2009): 195-202. Web. 11 Oct. 2010.

Harris, Jessica B. "The Culinary Seasons of My Childhood." *Gastropolis: Food and New York City.* Eds. Annie Hauck-Lawson & Jonathan Deutsch. New York: Columbia UP, 2008. 108-115.

"Moe's SW Grill." http://www.moes.com. Moe's Southwest Grill 2009. Web. 11 Oct. 2010.

Niman, Nicolette Hahn. "The Carnivore's Dilemma." *New York Times* 31 Oct. 2009, NY ed., A21. Web. 11 Oct. 2010.

Paarlberg, Robert. "Attention Whole Foods Shoppers." *Foreign Policy.* (May/June 2010): n. pag. Web. 10 Oct. 2010.

Piercy, Marge. "What's That Smell in the Kitchen?" *Circles on the Water: Selected Poems of Marge Piercy.* New York: Knopf Doubleday, 1982. 288. Print.

Powell, Julie. "Day 1, Recipe 1." *Julie & Julia: My Year of Cooking Dangerously.* New York: Little, Brown & Co., 2006. 3-23. Print.

Salatin, Joel. "Declare Your Independence." *Food, Inc.* New York: Public Affairs, imprint of Perseus Books, 2009. 183-196. Print.

Scully, Matthew. "Fear Factories: The Case for Compassionate Conservatism –for Animals." *The American Conservative.* 23 May 2005. n. pag. Web. 11 Oct. 2010.

Sedaris, David. "Tasteless." *New Yorker.* 3 Sept. 2007. n. pag. Web. 11 Oct. 2010.

Townsend, Elisabeth. "The Cooking Ape: An Interview with Richard Wrangham." *Gastronomica: The Journal of Food and Culture.* 5.1 (Winter 2005): 29-37. Web. 11 Oct. 2010.

Waters, Alice. "A Healthy Constitution." *The Nation.* 289,8 (21 Sept. 2009): 11-15. Web. 11 Oct. 2010.

"A Woman's Place?" *New York Magazine* 40.38 (29 Oct. 2007): 54-58. Web. 11 Oct. 2010.